1

The Great Bride Awakening

DR. NOVA DEAN PACK

The Great Bride Awakening
1st Printing - Version II
Copyright © 1995 - Dr. Nova Dean Pack
Revised Copyright 2023 - Dr. Nova Dean Pack

Photos used by attribution;
photo by wirestock
photo by YuriArcursPeopleimages
photo by YuriArcursPeopleimages
photo by wirestock
photo by YuriArcursPeopleimages
photo by YuriArcursPeopleimages
photo by Jamet Lene on Unsplash
photo by YuriArcursPeopleimages
photo by YuriArcursPeopleimages
photo by astrakanimages
photo by monkeybusiness
photo by Freepik
photo by wirestock
photo by Agalokos
photo by LightFieldStudios
photo by LightFieldStudios
photo by puhimec
photo by indypendenz
photo by YuriArcursPeopleimages
photo by wirestock
photo by wirestock
photo by wirestock

For permission requests, write to the publisher, addressed "Attention: Permissions" by electronic mail to:
packnovapack@aol.com

Scriptures taken from the New King James Version. Copyright © 1982 by Thomas Nelson, Inc. Used by permission. All rights reserved.

Scriptures quotations are from the King James Version (KJV) of the bible unless otherwise stated. Emphasis on certain scripture(s) is authors own.

Contents.

Contents.

Contents.

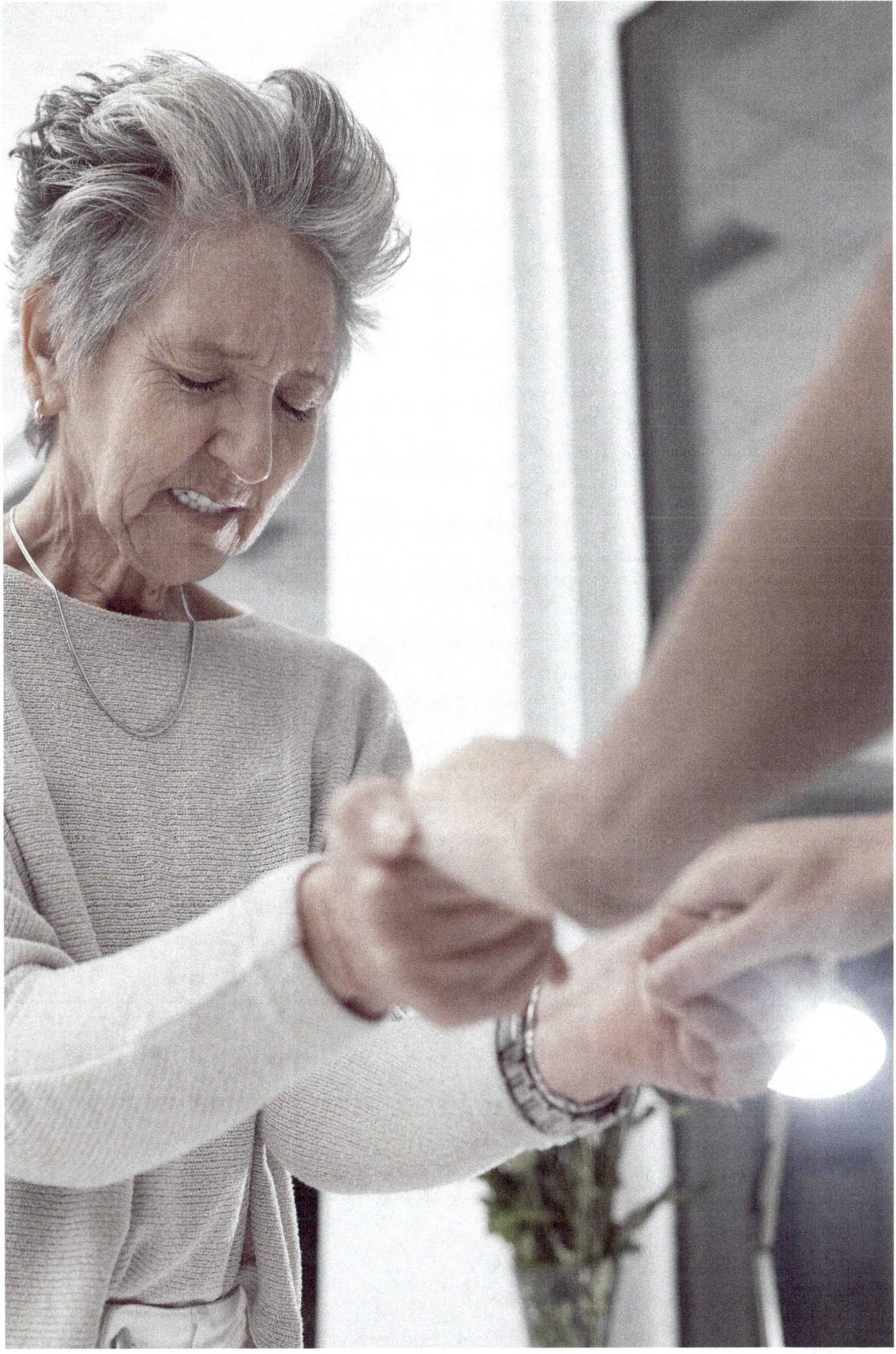

DEDICATION

I dedicate this book to the godly women in my family.

First and foremost, I dedicate this book to the most phenomenal woman of God that I have had the privilege of knowing, who has a Master's degree in education and counseling, along with two years of bible school. She is a constant encouragement to me. She is my wife, Linda Mundinger Pack. Her affirmations to me personally make me want to do better and seek deeper the greater spiritual ideas, thoughts, and wisdom from the Bible and write them in teaching and book form. She is always there to give me time and space to pen the books the Holy Spirit leads me to write. My wonderful godly wife is my best friend and godly companion. Every morning is our personal Bible study together.

Next, I want to dedicate this book to my mother, Bonita Aldridge Pack, who before her untimely death at age 32 in 1959, spoke the greatest affirmation to me when I was just 10 years old. She told me, "Although God made you very smart, you must remember that God brought you back from death for a special reason when you were just 90 days old. Regardless, what you accomplish in life, you owe Jesus for your life; so, serve Him with your whole heart." This affirmation, and her memory, has motivated me in my spiritual walk my entire life.

Then, I would like to dedicate this book to a very godly woman of God, my daughter, Destiny Faith Pack, who has overcome great obstacles in her life, has a degree in ministry, and has been prophesied by Kim Clement under the anointing of the Holy Spirit that Destiny will be a great spiritual leader for her generation.

Next, I want to dedicate this book to my sister Bonnie Pack Coffman. My sister is a great woman of God. She is a servant and loves people. She studies her Bible, but what she learns she puts into action. Bonnie is always helping someone in need. After our mother died, Bonnie tried her best to fill the void of our absent mother, and she helped her siblings endure life, even though it was harsh. Bonnie was a great strength for my sister, Joyce, now deceased, and my three brothers, Ronnie, Roger, and Danny, now deceased. Bonnie is a very gifted painter, and she loves painting scenes of the Bible. Bonnie loves my teachings and writings, and she is always asking for more.

Finally, I dedicate this book to my two daughters-in-law, who are wonderful women of God, Jessica Pack and Michelle Pack. Each of these wonderful women of God have a Master's degree, with Jessica having a Master's degree in education while Michelle having a Master's degree in psychology, who also has a Marriage Family Child Counseling license. Jessica is married to my son, Brandon, and Michelle is married to my son, Joshua. These women bring a Christian foundation in their marriages and in their homes which they are teaching to their children. My sons are truly blessed of the Lord for having such godly women as their wives.

With all my love,

Nova

Introd

uction

INTRODUCTION

This book is written to bring to light that Christ Jesus brought a new social order where the privileges and priorities based upon male and female were discarded as to Believers.

When I originally researched and sought the Holy Spirit on this subject, it was at the request of Pastor Rebekah Rodriguez in San Bernardino county, California, who herself is a Mexican American Woman Pastor. She was having problems with the men in her congregation accepting her authority as a Pastor because she was a woman; and she asked me to study the problem and minister to the men, who were invited to attend a special women's meeting for this purpose to hear what I had to say. In this gathering, several of the men in her Ekklesia congregation did not believe that God gave spiritual authority to a woman Pastor to minister to men.

When I finished ministering the foundational basis of this word, (which has since been expanded into this book) one hundred percent of all the men present at this meeting were convicted and came forward for repentance, deliverance, or to confess that they now believed that according to scripture women can be Ephesians 4:11 Ministers. What I taught from scriptures that day caused them radically to change the foundations of their beliefs.

The American Standard Version correctly translates Galatians 3:28 to say, "There can be neither Jew nor Greek, there can be neither bond nor free, there can be no male and female; for ye all are one man in Christ Jesus." Most English translations inaccurately translate the third clause as "There is neither male nor female." However, the pure Greek rendering that denotes the series of neither...nor is broken by the conjunctive and, which suggests that the better translation would read "male and female" instead of "neither male nor female." The New American Standard Version gives the conjunctive "and" rendering, but only in the margin as an alternative translation.

Similarly, Colossians 3:11 proclaims the same liberty of the gospel which was not seen before: "Where there is neither Greek nor Jew, circumcised nor uncircumcised, Barbarian, Scythian, slave nor free, but Christ is all and in all." However, since there is no difference between men and women in the Kingdom of God, no distinction was provided in this verse.

Different social distinctions in the natural are listed in the Bible using the words "neither . . . nor." On the other hand, male and female form a unity of oneness in the Bible unlike the other cultural distinctions which are always contrasting opposites. You cannot be Greek and Jew or slave and free in the natural, but in the spirit you can. For example, men can give birth in the spiritual realm to spiritual revelations; both men and women can be circumcised in their hearts. A person can have liberty but also be a doulos unto the Lord. Gender types do not increase or decrease the blessings, privileges, duties, or priorities in the spiritual Kingdom of God.

Jesus acknowledged the oneness of the male and female in Mark 10:6: "But from the beginning of the creation, God made them male and female."

God did not say He made them male or female. The conjunctive was used to describe the oneness of male and female, and additionally to show that each person has male and female functions inside of them, which will be discussed later.

Every Jewish male was taught that because of the Jewish oral law, he should thank God daily that he had not been made a Gentile, a slave, or a woman. In Galatians 3:28 above, Paul addressed this Jewish oral tradition and declared the start of a new social order where the privileges and priorities based on the distinctions of male and female, and traditionally other distinctions, were discarded.

Under the Jewish law, males had greater privileges and priorities than the females. For example, only males were circumcised, which was the sign of the Abrahamic Covenant. On the other hand, baptism of Believers applies to both male and female. Under the Jewish law, only males could be kings and priests. Both males and females are kings and priests in the Kingdom of God through Christ Jesus (Revelation 1:6). Under the Jewish law, only males were entitled to prior privileges to inheritances. In the New Testament women Believers are joint heirs with the men Believers in Christ Jesus (Romans 8:17; 1 Peter 3:7). In the resurrection, the sexual relation of the sexes shall cease (Luke 20:35). Accord-

ingly, the distinctions of religious offices and social ranks based upon gender are extinguished in Christ's spiritual Kingdom.

Men and women who are Believers are equal citizens of heaven (Philippians 3:20), equal members of the body of Christ, equally employed as members of the spiritual Ekklesia Kingdom government as spiritual Ambassadors of Christ (1Corinthians 5:20), equally employed as members of the spiritual Ekklesia Kingdom Army as spiritual Soldiers (2 Timothy 2:3-4). Men and women who are Believers are both commanded to seek first the Kingdom of God and His righteousness (Matthew 6:33). Men and women who are Believers are both called to preach the gospel of the Kingdom (Matthew 24:14) and the repentance and remission of sins (Luke 24:47). Men and women who are Believers are gifted by God the Father (Romans 12:6-8), gifted by God the Word/Son (Ephesians 4:11), and/or gifted by God the Holy

Spirit (1 Corinthians 12:8-10).

With Christ Jesus came freedom of women for the sake of preaching the gospel of the Kingdom and repentance and remission of sins throughout Israel and all Gentile nations and cultures. The New Testament is full of men and women used and treated as complementary, harmonious, and equal Ministers.

Likewise, Jesus gave blessings to men and women without distinction or preference. The song of Jesus' mother, Mary, followed the song of John the Baptist's father, Zacharias. Both the man Simeon and the woman Anna prophesied over the baby Jesus in the temple when He was brought to the Temple to be circumcised. Jesus' conversation with Nicodemus in John 3 was followed by Jesus' conversation with the Samaritan woman at the well in John 4. Peter's pronouncement in John 6: 69 that Jesus is the Christ is followed by Martha's pronouncement in John 11:27 that "Yes, Lord, I believe that You are the Christ, the Son of God, who is to come into the world." In John 6:6-10 the man with a withered hand was healed on the Sabbath. In Luke 13:10-13, the woman who was bowed with an infirmity also was made whole on the Sabbath. In the New Testament, male and female Believers were raised from the dead, healed, while others were disciples that were used strongly in ministry. The woman caught in adultery was not condemned by Jesus, but the men who were trying to judge her (but not the man caught in adultery) under the law were themselves convicted of sin

(John 8:3-12). Living in a male dominated society, Jesus honored and liberated the women from bondage of religious tradition and Jewish culture through illumination of His way, truth, and life in His Kingdom.

Christ's message of the gospel of the Kingdom and the message of repentance and remission of sins freed women everywhere the disciples went in the world. Under Gentile culture the women were second- or third-class citizens, or designated as mere chattel. Hence, Christianity was very popular amongst the women in these Eastern and Mid-Eastern cultures, as Christianity gave women a status theretofore never experienced on a widespread basis. Yet, there were occasional abuses of the liberty afforded wives as new Believers, which Apostle Paul addressed to bring order to the Church, as will be seen in this book.

Truly, the spiritual emancipation of women is secondary to or parallel with the emancipation of all mankind from the bondage of the law of sin and death unto the freedom of the law of the Spirit of life in Christ Jesus (Romans 8:2). Accordingly, women who are saved are liberated from bondage of a fallen world the same as men, the same as Greeks or Jews, the same as slave or free. Acceptance of Jesus as Lord and Savior after the gospel of the Kingdom is preached and repentance and remission of sins which liberates everyone in Christ's Spirit, regardless of culture, race, status, or gender. "Now the Lord is the Spirit; and where the Spirit of the Lord is there is liberty" (2 Corinthians 3:17).

Dr. Nova Dean Pack

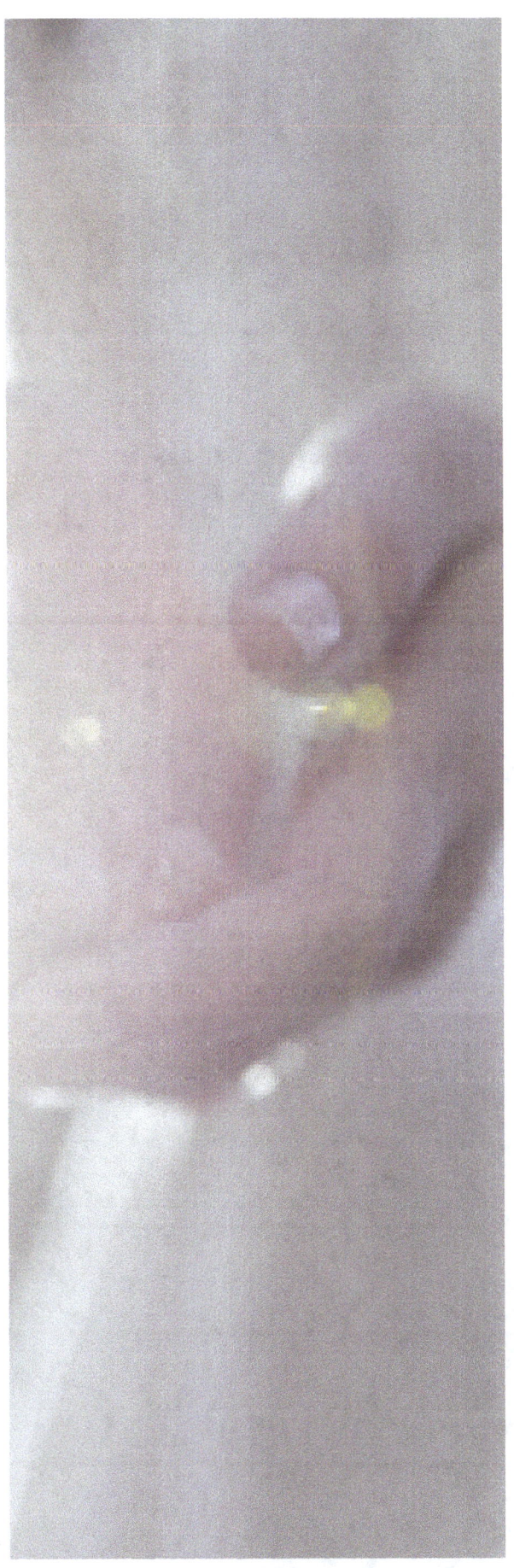

God created the Woman equal to the Man

Chapter One

CHAPTER ONE

GOD CREATED THE WOMAN EQUAL TO THE MAN

To bring liberty to women to become Ephesians 4:11 Ministers, the issues raised by Genesis, chapters 1, 2, and 3 will reveal the origin of the historical bias of men religious leaders and so-called scholars that interpreted scripture in a way that falsely disqualified women from leadership ministry.

Genesis 1:26-28 pronounces God's creative design and purpose for mankind, both man and woman. "Then God said, 'Let Us make man in Our image, according to Our likeness; let them (both male and female) have dominion over the fish of the sea, over the birds of the air, and over the cattle, over all the earth and over every creeping thing that creeps on the earth. 'So, God created man in His own image; in the image of God, He created him; male and female He created them. Then God blessed them, and God said to them, 'Be fruitful and multiply; fill the earth and subdue it; have dominion over the fish of the sea, over the birds of the air, and over every living thing that moves on the earth.'"

Genesis 1:28 is the foundational dominion mandate that both men and women Believers are commissioned by God to fulfill. The Hebrew word for dominion in Genesis 1:26, 28 is mamlaka, (Strongs H4467), which comes from the primitive root words malak (Strongs H4427), melek (Strongs H4428), or mashal (Strongs H4910). These are the same or similar Hebrew words that are translated into English as kingdom (Exodus 19:6), reign (Exodus 15:18), King (Genesis 14:8), rule (Judges 8:22), and realm (2 Chronicles 20:30). All these Hebrew words are related to the Kingdom of God being established here on earth. God granted dominion authority to both men and women Believers for them to exercise this authority to share His Kingdom and creative goodness throughout the world. God's ultimate purpose was for men and women to multiply and fill the earth as the multi-Believers Betrothed and Bride of God's only begotten Son, Jesus, who would come to earth in the future in God's own timing (Galatians 4:4).

Genesis 5:2 in the King James version asserts, "... In the day that God created man, He made him in the likeness of God. Male and female created He them; and blessed them, and called their name adam, in the day they were created." In the Amplified version Genesis 5:2 emphasizes that both male and female were called adam. "He created them male and female and blessed them and named them [both] adam at the time when they were created."

Apparently, both the male and female were called adam and adam which meant man and man prior to the fall, and the male adam was later called Adam and the female adam was later named Eve by Adam after the fall according to Scripture (Genesis 3:20).

In the perfect state in the Garden of Eden before the fall, the equality of the genders was present. Likewise, it is interesting that the Bible often uses what appears to be the male gender, adam, in Hebrew and man in English when referring to the generic human race. The Genesis 5:2 explanation devastates the secular feminist's statement that the Bible is a sexist book, especially since in His triune nature God also is referred to by the male gender pronoun, He. In the same vein the word, adam is used to mean humanity in its generic sense, and in Numbers 31:35 adam is used in the Scripture to refer exclusively to women.

As will be seen, every man and woman functions with both male and female genders features. The spirit and soul were created immortal, and the body was created mortal. Yet, the spirit and body were created to function as male genders to give stimuli to the soul, consisting of the mind, emotions, and heart, where man's Will resides, were created to function as female genders to receive stimuli from the two counterparts of the male adam and female adam, the spirit and body. The spirit brings spiritual stimuli to the soul while the body through its five senses brings natural stimuli to the soul.

The word, man in Genesis 5:2 also is the generic word used for mankind or humanity, with the male and female called adam and adam in the Hebrew. Hence, both male adam and female adam were made in the image and likeness of God, not just the male adam. Likewise, God never said that the male adam or female adam originally was created to have dominion over another male adam or female adam which would be born as children of the first male adam and first female adam. Enslavement of any male adam or female adam is against God's creative design and purpose which was to give mankind free will to make decisions and choices. Both the male adam and female adam were given dominion authority jointly over the things of the earth in the original creation order, not just the male adam. Thus, God saw them both as equals in granting to them authority and power. Genesis 1:27-28 says, "So God created man in His own image, in the image of God created He him; male and female created He them. (28) And God blessed them, and God said unto them, 'Be fruitful, and multiply, and replenish the earth, and subdue it: and have dominion over the fish of the sea, and over the fowl of the air, and over every living thing that moveth upon the earth.'" The dominion mandate was granted to both the male Adam and the female Adam.

Colossians 1:15-17 says, "Who (Jesus) is the image of the invisible God, the firstborn of every creature: (16) For by Him were all things created, that are in heaven, and that are in earth, visible and invisible, whether they be thrones, or dominions, or principalities, or powers: all things were created by Him, and for Him. And He is before all things, and by Him all things consist." Jesus' divine nature, God the Word, was actively involved in creating the spiritual and natural worlds. Jesus' humanity nature was the express image of God and was used as the pattern and design to create the natural and spiritual worlds.

Thus, the humanoid image and likeness that was used as a pattern or design to create the male adam and female adam was already in existence, and that humanoid (God's only begotten Son) had both a divine nature and humanity nature that was not commingled and was all God and all man in His two natures. His

Sinless Seed finite form was the only begotten Son of the invisible infinite God, and the only begotten Son was living in the bosom of God the Father (John 1:18) before anything in the spiritual and natural worlds were created.

Hebrews 11:3 says, "Through faith we understand that the worlds were framed by the word of God, so that things which are seen were not made of things which do appear." 1 Peter 1:20 proclaims, "He (Christ's humanity nature) indeed was foreordained before the foundation of the world but was made manifest in these last times for you who through Him believe in God Who raised Him from the dead and gave Him glory, so that your faith and hope are in God." Hebrews 1:2 states, "(God) has in these last days spoken to us by His Son; Whom He has appointed Heir of all things, through whom also He made the worlds." Jesus Christ, with His dual natures, pre-existed the creation of the spiritual and natural worlds, but inside the humanity nature of God's only begotten Son was the pattern by which God created the spiritual and natural worlds. Jesus said in John 17:5 "And now, O Father, glorify Thou Me with Thine own Self with the glory which I had with Thee before the world was."

Since the only begotten Son of the Father was the first finite Person in existence, and Who was slain from the foundation of the world in God's eternal spiritual realm (Revelation 13:8), Believers could be chosen to be in Christ before time began and before the worlds were created. 2 Timothy 1:9 declares, "(God) has saved us (men and women) and called us (men and women) with a holy calling not according to our works, but according to His own purpose and grace which was given to us in Christ Jesus before time began." Ephesians 1:4–5 says, "According as He hath chosen us in Him before the foundation of the world, that we should be holy and without blame before Him in love: (5) Having predestinated us unto the adoption of children by Jesus Christ to Himself, according to the good pleasure of His will." 1 Peter 1:23 asserts, "Having been born again, not of corruptible seed, but Incorruptible (Seed Who is Christ Jesus' sinless resurrected humanity nature), through the Word of God (Christ's divine nature) which lives and abides forever."

I believe reason dictates that the first male adam's body was originally created without a particular exclusive gender in the natural, as he apparently was both male and female because the female portion was taken out of him by God in creating his spouse, the female adam. The female adam, too, had a triune nature in the image and likeness of God. The male adam and female adam were each created with a triune nature, with each nature having either a male function or a female function. Like God, the male adam and female adam were created with fully functioning vibrant human spirits, along with souls that had thoughts in their minds, feelings in their emotions, and beliefs in their hearts, where their wills reside to make choices as free moral agents, unlike animals who are propelled more by instincts then intelligence (Matthew 10:31).

The man and woman were created by God as moral beings that were spiritually conscious in their spirits, self-conscious in their souls, and sensory conscious in their bodies; and each part of mankind was to function in righteous obedience according their creative function. The body and the soul of both the man and woman were designed by God to assist the spirit to dominate the world with God's granted dominion authority and power under the direct authority, empowerment, enablement, instruction, and supervision of God (Genesis 1:26-28). Unlike God Almighty, the man and woman were not the Creator of the world, and all that was in it. Unlike God Almighty, the man and woman were not infinite, omnipresent, omnipotent, immutable, or omniscient. Instead, man and woman were finite and limited in their authority and power and received their subsistence and life by the will, authority, power, and love of God. God equally cared for the man and woman that He created, not just the man. Both the man and woman had equal importance with God.

Man and woman came from God's heart essence, were created for God's relationship and glory, and were designed to remain as loving and working companions of God eternally, along with God's only begotten Son once He came to earth with His chosen body (Isaiah 43:7; Ephesians 2:10; Revelation Ch. 21). Since man and woman came from God's heart, God loves man and woman and still expresses that love. The first Man and Woman were both God's masterpiece of all creation as man, both male and female, came from and were patterned after the Master, Himself, Christ's humanity nature in sinless seed form Who was and became the manifested Word made flesh in the fullness of time (Psalm 139:13-16; John 1:1-5, 14, 15; Galatians 4:4).

Unlike the unaffectionate brute creation of animals, man and woman were created beings in the image and likeness of God and with whom God could commune in love and fellowship, who in turn could reciprocate God's love (1 John 4:16-19). Psalms 8:5 teaches, "For You have made Him (man, woman, and the humanity nature of Jesus) a little lower than the angels (Hebrew Elohim which refers to the Triune Nature of God or heavenly angelic beings), and You have crowned Him with glory and honor." Man in the generic sense, both male and female, was created to protect, dominate, cultivate, and care for the world under the direct supervision of God (Genesis 1:26, 28).

Why did God form the immortal male functioning spirit of the man and woman before the fall? God formed the original immortal male functioning spirit of the man and woman in His image and likeness since God is Spirit and the Father of all spirits (Numbers 16:22; John 3:6; John 4:24; Hebrews 12:9). The immortal male functioning spirit has the vital life power from God to distinguish the living from the dead. God formed the immortal female functioning soul from the immortal male functioning spirit; so, the immortal female functioning soul also was created in the immortal image and likeness of God and out of man's immortal male functioning spirit (Genesis 2:7). Zechariah 12:1 proclaims, "The burden of the word of the LORD for Israel, saith the LORD, which stretcheth forth the heavens, and layeth the foundation of the earth, and formeth the spirit of man within him." The word man is used in the generic sense as pertaining to both male man and female man, which is the man and woman; but the immortal male functioning spirit communed in the spiritual realm.

Since generic man's primary essence is a spirit, although he has a soul, and lives in a body, only the spirit of generic man knows whether his spirit and soul are going to exist infernally or eternally. 1 Corinthians 2:11 says, "For what man knoweth the things of a man save the spirit (Greek - pneuma) of a man which is in him? Even so the things of God knoweth no man, but the Spirit of God." Likewise, 1 Corinthians 2:14 maintains, "But the natural (Greek - psuchikos) man receiveth not the things of the Spirit of God; for they are foolishness unto him; neither can he know them, because they are spiritually (Greek - pneumatikos) discerned."

In the original creation, man and woman were created with a triune nature in the image of God. 1 Thessalonians 5:23 says, "And the very God of peace sanctify you wholly; and I pray God your whole spirit and soul and body be preserved blameless unto the coming of our Lord Jesus Christ."

The body of the man and body of the woman had different functions, primarily because of the God-created purpose of the woman as the child bearer and nourisher of children while the man was primarily the provider for the family as a farmer and laborer in the physical environment, although historically women worked in the fields as well. In both man and woman, they had an immortal female functioning soul, consisting of the mind, emotions, and heart, where the will resides. However, in the spiritual realm, the man and woman functioned the same way because both were created as having an immortal male functioning spirit.

To explain with easier understanding, I will discuss how God originally created the spirit, soul, and body of Adam and Eve to function as different genders, with the spirit being a male giver of stimuli from the spiritual world, and the body being a male giver of stimuli through his five senses from the natural world, while the soul was created as a receiver of spiritual stimuli from the spirit or natural stimuli through the five senses of the body.

The spirit and soul were created as immortals, while the body was created as a mortal. I will refer in this discussion pertaining to the creation of humankind, to the spirit as the immortal male functioning spirit or once saved the immortal male functioning born again spirit. I will refer to the soul as the immortal female functioning soul. I will refer to the body as the mortal male functioning body.

Spirit: Scripture reveals that the immortal male functioning spirit was created, and when born again through Christ Jesus, to function as a male gatherer and giver of spiritual world stimuli in man's creative triune nature. Colossians 3:10 says, "And have put on the new man (immortal male functioning born again spirit), which is renewed in knowledge after the image of Him that created him." The immortal male functioning spirit was created to commune with God in the spiritual realm, and the new, immortal male functioning born again spirit of the Believer is the new man and new creature in Christ, and he had/has the duty to daily bring spiritual nourishment to the immortal female functioning soul with spiritual stimuli, defined as spiritual thoughts, spiritual feelings, and spiritual heartfelt beliefs.

Soul: The immortal female functioning soul was created to function as the receiver of stimuli in man's created triune nature because the immortal female functioning soul is receptive of thoughts in the mind, feelings in the emotions, and beliefs in the heart. David said in Psalm 34:2, "My SOUL shall make her boast in the Lord…" The Hebrew word for soul is the Hebrew feminine nephesh.

In Psalms 22:20, David also said, "Deliver my SOUL from the sword; my darling from the power of the dog." In Psalms 35:17 David said, "Lord, how long wilt thou look on? Rescue my soul from their destructions, my darling from the lions." In these two Psalms, David refers to his soul as "my darling." The word darling in the Hebrew is the feminine yâchıyd, meaning beloved, lonely, or darling. In these Psalms, the Hebrew clearly shows that David meant his soul to function as a female gender; so, the Hebrew properly translated was the soul functioning with a female gender when David referred to his soul as "her boast in the Lord" and "my darling."

Some religious traditionalists may question this gender functioning distinction in Scripture between the spirit, soul, and body, especially my teaching and common usage of the immortal female functioning soul. So, let us study Scripture to confirm this illuminating truth. We all know that the Earth, for example, is referred to as having a female function, as Mother Earth. The reason is that whatever you plant in Mother Earth in seed form starts germinating, growing, and maturing into a plant or tree. Thus, Mother Earth is God's created receiver and is always being receptive, growth encouraging, and reproductive in function.

Similarly, in the parable of the four soils, the seed is the word of the Kingdom, and the heart in the immortal female functioning soul is the ground where the word of God's Kingdom in seed form is planted for new life, growth, fruitbearing, and multiplication. Matthew 13:19 says, "When any one heareth the word of the kingdom, and understandeth it not, then cometh the wicked one, and catcheth away that which was sown in his heart. This is he which received seed by the wayside." The word of the Kingdom is always perfect, righteous, and holy, but it is the condition of the ground in the four soils that makes the difference where you receive a 30-, 60-, or 100-fold return. The biblical seed is the word of God's Kingdom planted in the heart in the immortal female functioning soul, just as a seed is planted in Mother Earth, which was created by God as female in nature. Likewise, it is the condition of the heart in the soul where the word of the kingdom is planted that determines the 30-, 60-, or 100-fold return.

Once saved, the immortal male functioning born again spirit, under the perfect submission to the Holy Spirit, continuously brings the word of God's Kingdom from the spiritual world and plants the word of God's Kingdom in the heart to transform the immortal female functioning soul. The heart also has a functioning female gender in the creative design of God as being receptive, growth encouraging, and reproductive in function.

Similarly, 1 Peter 1:13 says, "Wherefore gird up the loins of your mind, be sober, and hope to the end for the grace that is to be brought unto you at the revelation of Jesus Christ" The loins are referencing the immortal female functioning soul where reproduction occurs once the seeds, as words, are planted in the mind, emotions, or heart. The mind functions as a female receiver. If the seed is a word from the flesh, fallen world, or kingdom of darkness, then it is planted in the mind as tares. The word, idea, image, or sound that are tares are planted in the mind starts germinating, growing, and reproducing there; so, Peter is warning the Believers to protect their minds from the intrusion of fleshly, worldly, or evil thoughts. The mind in the immortal female functioning soul is very receptive, so, the Believer must close the gates of the mind and train the mind to have discernment to distinguish the difference between the word seeds that are either wheat or tares. On the other hand, the word of the Kingdom (Matthew 13:19) is planted in the heart as good wheat and not tares.

God's Kingdom wisdom is female in function and transforms the immortal female functioning soul. Proverbs 2:4 says, "If thou seekest her (wisdom) as silver, and searchest for her as for hid treasures." A Believer's immortal female functioning soul should receive wisdom from above, not earthly wisdom (James 3:17). God's wisdom encourages Kingdom growth, reproduces Kingdom thoughts, Kingdom instructions, Kingdom truths, Kingdom patterns for life, Christ's image, and Kingdom worship sounds, Kingdom thoughts in the mind, Kingdom feelings in the emotions, and Kingdom beliefs in the heart that are planted there by the immortal male functioning born again spirit from God's Kingdom by the leading of the Holy Spirit for transformation, comfort, and wisdom of the immortal female functioning soul.

Wisdom in the Bible is always referred to as feminine in function. The word wisdom is the Hebrew female word chokmali (Proverbs 8:5) and is the Greek female word sophia. 1 Corinthians 1:24 refers to Jesus' female functioning soul as manifested Wisdom. "But unto them which are called, both Jews and Greeks, Christ the power of God, and the wisdom (sophia) of God."

Women Believers are often more apt to find the transformation and sanctification of their immortal female functioning souls as a lifestyle of manifested righteousness, holiness, and wisdom seeking first to enter and staying in God's Kingdom as their place of service, intimacy with the Lord, and sanctuary from the fallen world.

Body: The mortal male functioning body was created to function as a giver to the immortal female function soul of natural world stimuli in man's creative triune nature. The mortal male functioning body was originally designed by God to be the butler for the immortals, and the mortal male functioning body's job was to regulate what comes in through the five senses from the four-dimensional physical world of height, width, depth, and time. Romans 6:6-7 says, "Knowing this, that our old man (body and flesh) is crucified with Him, that the body of sin might be destroyed that henceforth we should not serve sin. For he that is dead is freed from sin."

The immortal male functioning spirit and immortal female functioning soul were created from God's breath. God formed man's immortal male functioning spirit from God's breath (spirit), and God formed man's immortal female functioning soul from man's immortal male functioning spirit. God formed man's mortal male functioning body from the dust of the ground. In the King James version, Genesis 2:7 teaches, "And the Lord God formed (yatsar) man (adam) of the dust of the ground (adamah) and breathed (naphach) into his nostrils the breath (neshamah-divine inspiration or spirit) of life (chay); and man became a living (chay) soul (nephesh)." The New King James, New American Standard, New International, and Amplified versions all translate the second part of this Scripture as "… and man became a living being."

The Hebrew word for breath is neshamah, which is often interpreted as spirit. Proverbs 20:27 conveys, "The spirit (neshamah) of man is the candle of the Lord searching all the inward part of the belly." Likewise, Job 26:4 says, "To whom hast thou uttered words? And whose spirit (neshamah) came from Thee." Job 32:8 also affirms, "But there is a spirit (roach- breath, wind) in man and the inspiration (neshamah - breath) of the Almighty giveth them understanding."

When God breathed into Adam's nostrils the breath of life, Adam became a living immortal male functioning spirit and a living immortal female functioning soul. That which is living came from the spirit, as life is in the spirit. Adam's immortal female functioning soul came into existence because the immortal male functioning spirit was created by God's breath. Accordingly, it was the first man's immortal male functioning spirit which was designed by God to give life to man's immortal female functioning soul, not the other way around. God intended for man's immortal male functioning spirit to have headship over his immortal female functioning soul and his mortal male functioning body by spiritual knowledge, inspiration, wisdom, knowledge, understanding, and revelation from God. The mortal male functioning body was not created to have headship over the immortal female functioning soul or the immortal male functioning spirit, nor was the immortal female functioning soul made to rule over the immortal male functioning spirit. For either the mortal male functioning body or immortal female functioning soul to try to rule over the immortal male functioning spirit is an act outside the design and purpose of God.

God is Spirit, and God created a spiritual and physical universe for God, angels, other spiritual beings, and man and woman as God's image to live in, even though God and His angels and spiritual beings are not subject to the limitations of the physical earthly environment as are the man and woman. Notwithstanding, man and woman's immortal male functioning spirit was able to receive spiritual stimuli from the spiritual world.

Again, man and woman were created by God as each having an immortal male functioning spirit, from which came an immortal female functioning soul to live in a mortal male functioning body. The whole man and the whole woman lived within a physical environment, even though their immortal male functioning spirits were not subject to the limitations of the physical environment but were confined in the mortal male functioning body but could gather spiritual stimuli. The immortal male functioning spirits of man and woman could commune with those who lived in the spiritual world, especially God. Both man and woman were endowed with a free will to make choices by the heart in their immortal female functioning souls whether to serve the Kingdom of God or the kingdom of darkness.

2 Corinthians 4:10,11,16,18 declares, "Always carrying about in the body (soma) the dying of the Lord Jesus, that the life (zoe) of Jesus also may be manifested in our body (soma). For we who live (zao) are always delivered to death for Jesus' sake, that the life (zoe) of Jesus also may be manifested in our mortal flesh (sarx)…. Therefore, we do not lose heart. Even though our outward man is perishing (mortal), yet the inward man is being renewed day by day (immortal). …. While we do not look at the things which are seen, but at the things which are not seen. For the things which are seen are temporary (mortal), but the things which are not seen are eternal (immortal)." The inner man being renewed day by day is the immortal female functioning soul, which consists of the receptive mind, emotions and heart, where the will resides.

Like the immortal male functioning spirits and the immortal female functioning souls of both man and woman were formed by God and thus belong to God (Ezekiel 18:4). However, man and woman's mortal male functioning bodies were formed and made from the dust of the ground, and upon death will suffer decay back into the ground. The good news of the gospel of the Kingdom and the message of repentance and re-mission of sins is that Believers in the Lord Christ Jesus will in the future receive a new spiritual immortal male functioning body upon the Lord's return to earth (1 Corinthians 15:23, 42-44).

Even so, at time of creation, God had fashioned man and woman's mortal male functioning bodies to eventually become Temples of the entire Godhead. God formed the mortal male functioning body of the first man out of the earth (Genesis 2:7), itself; so, the man's mortal male functioning body would function as an earth suit, or better, as the home of the immortal male functioning spirit and immortal female functioning soul, and eventually as the Temple of the entire Godhead [1 Corinthians 3;16 (local church as Temple); 2 Corinthians 6:16 (individual as Temple); Ephesians 2:21 (universal Church as Temple)].

Apostle Paul revealed that man or woman's earthly mortal male functioning body is a seed, and upon death will be sown back into the ground as a natural, corruptible, dishonorable, mere dust but it will be raised a spiritual, incorruptible, glorious, powerful and immortal body (1 Corinthians 15:23, 35-38, 42-44).

It is a Believer's future hope that once a Believer is born again, the entire Godhead works to transform the soul, and the Believer will receive upon the Lord's return to earth a heavenly, incorruptible, glorified, powerful, and spiritual immortal body on resurrection day (I Corinthians 15:23). The new resurrected spiritual immortal male functioning body does not mean an immaterial body, but it will be made of a material adaptable to the new environment and realities of the new heaven and new earth in the age to come (Revelation 21:1). Resurrected man or woman will have a new spiritual immortal male functioning body like Christ Jesus which will be recognizable as a newly created generic man but will be able to dematerialize at any time and pass through closed doors or disguise himself like Jesus did (John 20:19,26; Luke 24:36). Resurrected man and woman's new spiritual immortal male functioning body will be made to carry out the will of God and the Lord Jesus Christ, as King, Lord, Priest of the Kingdom of God, whatever King Jesus decides, throughout eternity back here on earth when Christ returns (Revelation 21:3).

Genesis 2:18 proclaims, "And the Lord God said, 'It is not good that man should be alone; I will make him a helper comparable to him." Since the original man was both male and female, the female man that was taken out of the male man was comparable and complementary to the male man as his comparable and complementary helper. The actual Hebrew reads, "Lord God said not good man alone make helper (ezer) helper (ezer)." A helper or help meet are really two words in this scripture, and King James' translation of helpmeet as one word is inaccurate. The second use of the Hebrew word, ezer; denotes that the woman made by God was ideally suited or excellently fitted as the complementary helper of the man for the man's needs, completion, and jointly to carry forth God's mandate to be fruitful and multiply and subdue the earth.

The Hebrew word ezer comes from the Hebrew root word azar which means "to surround in aid, to protect, to help, to succor, to nourish, to care for, to sustain, to minister, and to love." The Hebrew word ezer was never meant to justify the placing of the woman in a lower class, subservient position, or unjustly subjugating her to enslavement, or treat her as mere chattel.

In truth, the Hebrew word ezer is used throughout Scripture to describe God, Himself, as the Helper (ezer) of man. Surely, one would never relegate God to a lower class just because He was said to be a Helper. For example, Deuteronomy 33:26 says, "There is no one like the God of Jeshurun, Who rides the heavens to help (ezer) you, and in His Excellency on the clouds." Psalm 33:20 likewise reveals, "Our soul waits for the Lord; He is our help (ezer) and our shield." Psalm 115:9-10 adds, "O Israel, trust in the Lord; He is their help (ezer) and their shield. O house of Aaron, trust in the Lord; He is their help (ezer) and their shield." Psalm 124:8 declares, "Our help (ezer) is in the name of the Lord, Who made heaven and earth."

Hence, since God, Himself, is called ezer, one cannot conclude that the word ezer signifies the placing of the woman in a lower position because she is designated as a helper. The woman like the man is to be a Christ-like servant to fulfill God's redemption Kingdom order and plan. Humility is a prerequisite to promotion. Also, both the man and woman are equal Kingdom Soldiers and equal Kingdom Ambassadors in God's Kingdom. Thus, the man and woman share equal authority in the Kingdom of God, and one is not subservient to the other, although everyone is submitted to being humble and subservient to the King of kings in the Kingdom of God.

Submission shows humility. Both men and women are to submit to God (James 4:7). Men and women have to submit to their employer. Both men and women are to submit to those who are spiritual leaders as they are helping them spiritually (1 Corinthians 16:16; Hebrews 13:17). All believers have to submit to the ordiances of government (1 Peter 2:13). Younger believers are to submit to elders, and everyone is to submit to each other, which includes men to spiritual women who have higher authority in church (1 Peter 5:5). Submission is part of humility: humility is prerequisite to promotion in the Kingdom of God (Philippians 2:5-9).

Genesis 2:22 states, "Then the rib which the Lord God had taken from man He made (banah) into a woman, and He brought her to the man." The Hebrew word, banah, means to build. In Genesis 2:7, the Scripture says the man was formed (yatsar) from the dust of the ground, but in Genesis 2:22 the Scripture differs in that God built the woman from the rib of the man. Genesis 2:18 also distinguishes man from woman in that God made or built (asah) woman instead of forming (yatsar) woman from the dust of the ground like He did the man. The Hebrew word asah means "making or providing something from substance that already exists."

The Hebrew word, asah was used in Genesis 1:7 which says, "Thus God made (asah) the firmament and divided the waters which were under the firmament from the waters which were above the firmament; and it was so." The firmament was asah from things on the earth already in existence. God merely rearranged it and divided it; so, it would no longer be without form and void. The word asah means "to make or provide order to the things in existence."

Therefore, when God made the woman, He brought order by a specially designed helper with whom man could have loving communion, companionship, support, and procreation. Again, man's complementary, comparable helper was asah and banah to bring wholeness, order, and completeness to the man.

Additionally, woman was made and built by God as man's complement, not man's competitor. Woman was to be man's joint helper to fulfill their joint mission given by God (Genesis 1: 26; 28). Accordingly, woman was joined to the man in submission to God to be the best team to fulfill God's mission of man and woman taking dominion and promoting God's Kingdom here on earth as it is in heaven.

Therefore, women are much, much more than just sex objects, door mats, baby making factorings, washing machines, or housekeepers. A woman is designed to complete a man, and together they are to make a family, home, and be God's Kingdom Ambassadors and Kingdom Soldiers here on earth as their joint ministry. Both man and woman have the same ministry call by God, not separate once married, but joined together in a complimentary manner where the togetherness is greater than each of their ministry calling, individually.

Both the man and woman were made in the image and likeness of God; so, to subjugate either the man or woman to be a slave human being is to violate God's creative design, mandate, and purpose. Any kind of slavery, diminution of rights, disrespect, use of force to control, abusive language, or humiliation, is not of God and is offensive to God; and the perpetrator of such diminution of the creative stature of the woman especially degrades the Betrothed of Christ and will receive the consequences of the wrongful actions against the Betrothed of God's only begotten Son.

God is still in the business of building the Woman (consisting of both men and women) as a comparable, complementary Betrothed for His only begotten Son, Christ Jesus, as He is the Son King of the Earth. God still uses that which is already in existence to asah and banah the Ekklesia, the multi-Believers Betrothed of Christ, the Ambassadors of Christ, the Soldiers of Christ, the Kings, Lords, and Priests here on earth submitted to the Godhead and the Lord Jesus Christ. 1 Corinthians 8:6 says, "But to us is but one God, the Father, of whom are all things, and we in Him, and one Lord Jesus Christ, by whom are all things and we by Him."

Jesus said in Matthew 16:18-19, "And I say also unto thee, 'That thou art Peter, and upon this rock I will build my Ekklesia (in context referring to an assembly of Soldiers, not an assembly of government representatives); and the gates of hell shall not prevail against it. (19) And I will give unto thee the keys of the kingdom of heaven: and whatsoever thou shalt bind on earth shall be bound in heaven: and whatsoever thou shalt loose on earth shall be loosed in heaven (bind and loose in this context refer to spiritual battle to bind the authority of the kingdom of darkness and loose the authority and blessing of God's Kingdom)."

God the Father, God the Word, and God the Holy Spirit, as one God, are still training and building Christ's Kingdom Ambassadors, Kingdom Soldiers, Kings, Lords, Priests, and Christ's Betrothed, using God's original building of the first Eve before the fall, and the second Eve (Believers as new creatures in Christ) as the pattern for the Ekklesia with delegated authority that God honored Jesus after His resurrection and in the future His coronation as King of kings and Lord of lords to rule and reign over all the Kingdoms here on earth (Matthew 28:18; 1 Timothy 6:15; Revelation 19:16; 11:15; 5:10).

Jesus' precious, sinless internal blood and internal water were shed when His side was pierced with a spear, when His blood and water were poured out onto the dust of the ground. John 19:34 says, "But one of the soldiers pierced His side with a spear, and immediately blood and water came out." Christ shed His precious blood and His precious eternal water for the cleansing that fell upon the ground from the wound in His side, along with His death, to create His Betrothed that also became His Ekklesia, who was His helper as the assembly of Kingdom Ambassadors assembly of Kingdom Soldiers, Kings, Lords, and Priests.

The Last Eve and Second Woman: Being asleep, the first Adam did not have to experience any pain to obtain his bride, but Jesus suffered much pain and death to obtain His Betrothed and later Bride because she was full of sin. In truth, men and women Believers as the Last Eve and Second Woman's new immortal male functioning born again spirit was made perfect, sinless, righteous, and holy; and the new immortal male functioning born again spirit is guarded by the entire Godhead living in man and woman's mortal male functioning body, which is the Godhead's Temple (Ephesians 4:24; 1 John 3:8). 1 John 5:18 says, "We know that whoever is born of God does not sin; but he who has been born of God keeps himself, and the wicked one does not touch him."

The first woman was built from the first man's rib, and the first man merely had to be put to sleep by God for the surgery to be done. The first Adam did not have to die to obtain his bride because he and his bride were innocent and had not yet sinned. God did not have to invoke His mandatory sentence of "dying you shall surely die" at the time God created the first Adam, not until Adam and Eve sinned (Genesis 2:7).

On the other hand, Jesus, as the Last Adam and Second Man was manifested here on Earth centuries after the first Adam had sinned; so, the Last Adam had to undergo God's mandatory sentence of death as the Sacrificial Lamb to become the Mediator to pay the price for His Betrothed as the helper of the Second Man, the last Adam, and as the Lord. The Ekklesia was not only to be the Last Eve and Second Woman, but also the New Creature and New Man in Christ that is made perfect, sinless, righteous, and holy (Hebrews 12:23; 1 Corinthians 15:45,47; 2 Corinthians 5:17; Ephesians 4:24).

The Lord declares in Matthew 16:18 that the gates (representing evil spiritual authorities) of Hades shall not prevail as the kingdom of darkness stronghold against Christ's Ekklesia, which in context are God's Kingdom Soldiers. Again, the Greek word, Ekklesia in Matthew 6:18 is a reference to the body of Christ as Kingdom spiritual soldiers fighting against the kingdom of darkness. Unlike the immortal male functioning born again spirit, the immortal female functioning soul must submit to a lifetime of transformation to become spiritually mature, righteous, and holy (Romans 12:2; Ephesians 4:24; Colossians 3:10). It is a continuous rejection by the soul of the flesh, the fallen world, and the Kingdom of darkness. It is a daily submission to God for the transformation of the soul.

Spiritual transformation of the mind, emotions, and heart of the immortal female functioning soul is the loving and disciplining labor of the entire Godhead toward the Last Eve and Second Woman. The mortal male functioning body of the Last Adam and Second Man and the Last Eve and Second Woman live inside each man and woman Believer, who individually, locally, and universally are God's Temple here on earth in side Believers (John 14:16,17,23; 1 Corinthians 3:16; 2 Corinthians 6:16; and Ephesians 2:21).

The Romans 12:2 transformation of the Soul: Romans 12:2 says about the immortal female functioning soul that: "And be not conformed to this world: but be ye transformed by the renewing of your mind, that ye may prove what is that good, and acceptable, and perfect, will of God."

The entire Godhead participates in the transformation of the immortal female functioning soul in both man and woman. God the Father prunes away the flesh's influence out of the Believer's immortal female functioning soul to bear more spiritual fruit (John 15:2). God the Word uses the rhema word of God to cleanse the dirty flesh out of the Believer's immortal female functioning soul and then sanctifies the immortal female functioning soul (Ephesians 5:26). God the Holy Spirit mortifies (kills) or starves the deeds of the flesh that are in the Believer's immortal female functioning soul to bring more zoe life (Romans 8:13).

The purpose of the immortal female functioning soul's spiritual transformation is "that she should be holy and without blemish" (Ephesians 5:27), so, she can commune in intimate relationship with the Godhead and Jesus' humanity nature as Lord. Jesus' humanity nature has been elevated by God with all authority in heaven and in earth and is the King of Kings, Lord of Lords, and High Priest of Priests in the order of Melchizedek (1 Timothy 6:15; Hebrews chapter 7; Revelation 1:6).

Ecclesiastes 3:11 proclaims an eternal goal of God: "He has made everything beautiful in its time. Also, He has put eternity in their hearts, except that no one can find out the work that God does from the beginning to now." God built into both woman and man beauty, so that man and woman can be attracted to each other. Likewise, God is building Christ's multi-Believers Betrothed and future Bride to be beautiful for Him; so, she will be attractive to Him when He returns to the earth after the marriage supper of the Lamb. Therefore, every Believer, both men and women must spend time at God's beauty parlor.

Romans 8:4-8 says of the mind in the immortal female functioning soul: "That the righteousness of the law might be fulfilled in us (men and women), who walk not after the flesh, but after the spirit. (5) For they (men and women) that are after the flesh do mind the things of the flesh; but they (men and women) that are after the spirit the things of the Spirit. (6) For to be carnally minded is death; but to be spiritually minded is life and peace. (7) Because the carnal mind is enmity against God: for it is not subject to the law of God, neither indeed can be. (8) So, then they (men and women) that are in the flesh cannot please God."

Woman was created by God with the same honor as the man. God bestowed on both the man and woman a high joint honor in His command for them "to be fruitful and multiply" and subdue and take dominion of the earth (Genesis 1:28). What God likes in His creation efforts, God blesses with multiplication instead of mere addition. Man and woman, jointly, were and are the only created spiritual beings allowed by God to participate through procreation (which means to consciously, emotionally, and believing that it is good to support the act of creation) of other spiritual human beings by their joining and becoming one.

Before Adam and Eve were created to participate with God by procreation to produce additional spiritual people, infinite God solely created angelic and other finite spiritual beings in the exercise of His sovereign will but were not created to produce other angelic beings. Even the devil was not given power to procreate and create another spiritual being. The devil can only deceive and steal the authority of man and woman who jointly were granted the privilege of aiding God in creating other spiritual beings.

Again, since the woman was made from the rib of the man's body (Genesis 2:21-22), the woman came from the essence and substance of the man, i.e., from the original oneness as part of God's creative design. "And Adam said, 'This is now bone of my bones and flesh of my flesh; she shall be called woman, because she was taken out of man'" (Genesis 2:23). Adam did not say blood of my blood because life in man is in his blood; and life originally came into man by the breath of God and put life in man's blood to nourish the physical life throughout the mortal male functioning body. Since life is in the blood, this is why sacrifice and shedding of innocent blood renders redemption through Christ's blood as a new covenant for the remission of sins to become born again to see God's Kingdom and to enter through being born of water and spirit to enter the Kingdom of God (John 3:3,5).

If man unlawfully subjugated the woman, he would be subjugating himself against the mandate of God for man and woman to stand in joint sovereign authority and jointly take dominion over the things on and of the earth. When the man looked at the woman, he saw part of himself. Therefore, like the man, the woman was made in the image and likeness of God in her spirit and soul which were immortal (Genesis 1:26-27) and like the man, the woman was made in her body in the likeness of the only begotten Son of God in sinless Seed form, Who at that time, was still in the bosom of the Father.

When the first male man's rib was surgically removed to build the first female man's spirit, soul, and body, the separate and distinct but complementary differences between the male man and female man were manifested. The female man received her immortal male functioning spirit and immortal female functioning soul also from the first male man; and the female man consequently had the same spiritual and soulish substance that was breathed into the nostrils of the first male man. Consequently, based upon creation attributes by God, the man and woman were created by God's own design to be equals.

The female man was called woman (from womb man) simply because she had a womb in her body, but her immortal male functioning spirit and immortal female functioning soul were exactly like the male man's immortal male functioning spirit and immortal female functioning soul. The female man's body was made by God to have the high honor of participating in the birth of spiritual beings, as only the man and woman creatures were mandated to be fruitful and multiply and procreate (support the creation) by giving birth to new spiritual human beings.

The female man also was called "fe male" because she would carry a fetus in her womb for nine months to create another spiritual and soulish human being. Angels cannot procreate or give birth to another spiritual angelic being, as this was reserved by God for the man and woman alone. In Genesis 1:28, "And God blessed them, and God said unto them, 'Be fruitful, and multiply, and replenish the earth, and subdue it: and have dominion over the fish of the sea, and over the fowl of the air, and over every living thing that moveth upon the earth.'" Consequently, the main difference between a man and woman is the mortal male functioning body as woman has a womb in which a fetus can grow once the egg of the female man is penetrated by the sperm or seed of the male man.

The woman is a man's equal, and she shares all of man's complementary authority, powers, faculties, dominion mandates, missions to subdue the things on earth, submitting to God's sovereign will, as joint heirs, and enjoying equal status in God's creative order.

When man saw woman, he saw himself, which ensured man's affection to protect and care for the newly made woman as from his own body. God's creation of the woman also ensured that the man would be stimulated to hold the woman in high esteem, not of a lower created order on a level with animals or treated as chattel. For a man to debase the woman was debasing himself because the woman was the man's complementary, harmonious counterpart, where their oneness manifested their wholeness and completeness, and especially created to jointly fulfill God's mission here on earth as Kings, Lords, and Priests, Ambassadors, and soldiers, and finally God's only begotten Son's Bride.

One of the favorite quotes read at weddings is from Matthew Henry, who said, "The woman was made of a rib out of the side of Adam; not made out of his head to rule over him, nor out of his feet to be trampled upon by him, but out of his side to be equal with him, under his arm to be protected, and near his heart to be beloved."

At time of creation, the immortal male functioning spirit of both the male man (Adam) and female man (Eve) was the head male in the man and woman, as the immortal male functioning spirit communed with God and took in spiritual stimuli from God's Kingdom and imparted that spiritual stimulus into the immortal female functioning soul, where the human mind, emotions, heart, and will reside. Colossians 3:10 instructs Believers, "And have put on the new man (immortal male functioning born again spirit), which is renewed in knowledge after the image of Him (Christ Jesus) that created him."

The mortal male functioning body of both the male man (Adam) and female man (Eve) was created by God to be the relegated subservient butler, which had five senses to send to the immortal female functioning soul the stimuli from the outside physical world.

Romans 6:6-7 says, "Knowing this, that our old man (body and flesh) is crucified with Him, that the body of sin might be destroyed that henceforth we should not serve sin. For he (body)that is dead is freed from sin."

The immortal female functioning souls of both the male man (Adam) and female man (Eve) have the minds, emotions, and hearts, where the wills reside; and their minds, emotions, hearts, and wills had and have a female function because the makeup of the immortal female functioning soul always is receptive to what is brought into the mind, emotions, and heart by either the immortal male functioning spirit or the mortal male functioning body.

The immortal female functioning soul was trapped in the middle and was unable to obtain stimuli herself from the spiritual world or the natural world that nourished or satisfied the immortal female functioning soul's desire for ideas, feelings, images, sounds, and beliefs; so, the immortal female functioning soul had and has to remain receptive until her mind, emotions, and heart convince either the immortal male functioning spirit or the mortal male functioning body to bring to the immortal female functioning soul the spiritual or natural stimuli she desires.

Again, in Psalm 34:2, David said, "My soul (nephesh, meaning soul, self, life, creature, person, mind, living being, emotions, heart, passion) shall make her boast in the Lord...." The male functioning parts of the man and woman (spirit and body) were to be givers to the immortal female functioning soul of spiritual stimuli or physical stimuli that each gathered from his sphere of influence and existence. Upon receipt, the immortal female functioning soul processes the spiritual or physical stimuli through her mind, emotions, and heart; and then she exercises her will to act in response to the stimuli.

Since the immortal female functioning soul had the mind, emotions, heart, and will, she had the creative authority that allowed her to exercise a decision of which kind of stimuli (spiritual or natural) to receive and use that benefited, nurtured, and stimulated the immortal female functioning soul for thoughts in her mind, feelings in her emotions, and beliefs in her heart. The immortal female functioning soul developed ideas, feelings, sounds, and images that became paintings, statutes, images, sounds that became music, and beliefs that established her guiding principles, philosophies, attitudes, ideas, viewpoints, images, politics, morals, and values that became the foundation of her existence and personality. The immortal female functioning soul sought after images and ideas in the spiritual world and the physical world that were adopted as a reason for living and purpose; and often these guiding principles, philosophies, attitudes, ideas, viewpoints, politics, images, morals, and values became idols against the commandments of God. Without God and His Kingdom, the immortal female functioning soul merely exists and does not enjoy life abundantly (John 10:10). Once the immortal female functioning soul finds Christ Jesus and accepts Him as Savior and Lord, then the immortal female functioning soul accepts and follows Jesus as the way, truth, and life personified (John 14:6).

The immortal male functioning spirit was the marital complementary head in God's Edenic Dominion Covenant (Genesis 1: 26-28); and with the immortal female functioning soul, like a marital counterpart helper, was commanded to steward and take dominion of all of God's creation on the earth, establish God's Kingdom, spread His creative goodness, and be fruitful and multiply. The immortal male functioning spirit's headship responsibility was to exercise loving authority to all functions of the total male man and total female man as foundationally a spiritual child of God.

The immortal male functioning spirit and the immortal female functioning soul were taken out of the essence and spiritual substance of God's breath, and thus were made immortal. Accordingly, the immortal male functioning spirit and immortal female functioning soul of both man and woman were equal in God's creative attributes as whole beings, with each standing before God in all creative dignity and glory with the same assignment to subdue the earth with the dominion Kingdom authority granted equally to both the man and woman, and to be fruitful and multiply to create more spiritual human beings.

The interests of the man and the woman were one and the same and were complementary to each other to fulfill God's dominion and multiplication mandates. The strong, physical characteristics of the man's mortal male functioning body were complemented by the tenderness, softness, and sympathy of the woman's mortal male functioning body. The man's mortal male functioning body was suited to provide and protect, while the woman's mortal male functioning body was endowed with maternal natures to birth and nurture new spiritual and soulish human beings. So, the woman's female functioning soul tended to complement the woman's mortal male functioning body to have affectionate closeness, emotional sensitivity, love, childbearing attentiveness, caring, and maintaining the health of the mortal male functioning body, as he was a vital part to carry the dominion and reproductive mandates of God.

The man and woman each had deficiencies and proficiencies that made up for what the other lacked; so, their needs of their mortal male functioning bodies to fulfill God's dominion and procreation mandate caused them to become one in relationship. Unfortunately, the woman did not have a child until after the fall, but at that time the immortal female functioning soul had a strained relationship with her mortal male functioning body because he was not immortal; but was always getting older and headed for death and decay back to dust. As will be revealed, her male functioning spirit went into a coma or a sleep-like death.

God is an agrarian: A farm is not complete unless it has its complement of land, crops, equipment, and livestock. Which is more important, the livestock, the crops, the equipment, or the land? All are needed to make a farm. Each of these things are important for a farm, and each helps the other. Crops are grown and are sold to third parties, and used to feed the livestock, which provides milk and food. The equipment and the land are needed to pasture the livestock, grow the crops, and the equipment are needed to prepare the soil and help harvest the crop when ripened, whether hay, vegetables, or fruit to feed livestock and family.

The point is the man and woman go together as an ice cube goes with a glass of water on a hot day. The man and woman go together like sun light and sun warmth. The man and the woman were made by God for each other, and the combination is better than the individual alone. Man and woman need each other's strengths to offset each other's weaknesses. Man and woman were made by God to be equal in person, in nature, in commission, in dignity, and in stature before God. Any enslavement, subjugation, or relegation to an inferior position of the woman by the man goes contrary to God's creative purpose and plan. A man is less effective without a woman, and a woman is less effective without a man.

How: The original family of God was the Father, Word, and Holy Spirit, and these three were-are one (1 John 5:7 - King James Version). Then, God gave birth to the only begotten Son of God and in the fullness of time He was named Jesus, Yeshua in Hebrew, or Yeshua HaMashiah (the proper name for Jesus Christ).

God is one family, and the family on earth is patterned after the family in God's kingdom. How could this be plainer than in the marriage oneness where the harmonious blend of the strengths and weaknesses start working in a single unit, being no more separate, but in the sacred institution of the family sanctioned and patterned after the family of God in His Kingdom (Ephesians 3:14-15). The Triune Godhead had a Son, named Jesus. Thus, parents with children is the family pattern.

Genesis 2:24-25 says, "Therefore a man shall leave his father and mother and be joined to his wife, and they shall become one flesh. And they were both naked, the man and his wife, and were not ashamed." Like the man, God made the woman not to be ashamed just because she was a woman, the weaker vessel in physical stature (1 Peter 3:7). God just made her more refined, more inclined to be able to see and administer over the more beautiful things of God's creation. In fact, the man should recognize that ". . . Woman is the glory of the man" (1 Corinthians 11:7). 1 Corinthians 11:11-12 concludes the thought: "Nevertheless, neither is man independent of woman, nor woman independent of man in the Lord. For as woman came from man, even so man also comes through woman, but all things are from God."

Man, and woman's mortal male functioning bodies were to be a willing, submissive, obedient type of butler who faithfully reported and guarded the door when things from the physical world tried to come into the house through one of the five entryways (senses). Therefore, the mortal male functioning body was a servant butler created to assist the immortal male functioning spirit and immortal female functioning soul to carry out their God-ordained joint purpose to take dominion of the physical world, with all three working together in harmonious interaction to do the will of God.

The Man
was more
culpable in
the fall

Chapter Two

CHAPTER TWO

The Man Was More Culpable in the Fall

Genesis 2:17 proclaims God's law spoken to Adam: "But of the tree of the knowledge of good and evil you shall not eat, for in the day that you eat of it you shall surely die." The actual literal rendering of the Hebrew is more accurate to read "...in the day you shall eat of it dying you shall surely die." There are two references to death in this Scripture in the Hebrew, dying and surely die.

The word dying is a reference to a process of death. The phrase surely die means immediate death. When Adam and Eve first sinned, their immortal male functioning spirits surely "died in sins" or went into a state of sleep like a coma, a living immortal death without dignity, function, consciousness of living, and without purpose. However, their mortal male functioning bodies only entered the process of dying. Every day, their mortal male functioning bodies had more death in them. For example, Adam's immortal female functioning soul, with the mind, emotions, and heart where the will lived, continued to function inside the mortal male functioning body, although his mortal male functioning body was experiencing the process of death, daily, until his final physical death at age 930 (Genesis 5:5).

Since both the male man and female man were called adam in Genesis 5:2, I sometimes will refer to them in a couple of chapters as the male adam and the female adam.

The male adam represents the headship immortal male functioning spirit in both the male adam and female adam, as God created the spirit in the female adam from the spirit in the male adam. The female adam was endowed with an immortal male functioning spirit, as a complementary helper to the male adam to take dominion over the entire earth and to multiply the male adam and the female adam's presence and influence on earth. The male adam and female adam together were drawn to the material world as their venue of ministry in God's Kingdom here on earth; and they both had fellowship with God in the cool of the evening concerning their stewardship duties in fulfilling the dominion mandate bestowed upon them by God (Genesis 1:26-28;3:8).

As finite beings, both the male adam and female adam had preoccupation with the material and natural finite world and with each other. Their perceptions of the importance of the natural finite world and each other eventually became the means of temptation that tainted and altered their discernment of God and

His infinite attributes as Creator. As a result of their sin of eating the forbidden fruit, God had to stop His fellowship as Father with both the male adam and female adam and had to become Judge.

Both the male adam and female adam developed through their five senses of their mortal male functioning bodies of things that were tangible in appearance. The male adam and female adam were developing the sin of covetousness for the acquisition of the knowledge what is good and evil of the natural world where God's glorious radiance covered natural creation were; and they did not understand that fallen good and evil were spiritual. The Tree of the Knowledge of Good and Evil and the Tree of Life were supernatural trees, not just finite trees as the other trees in the Garden of Eden, as they had infernal death and eternal life connected with them.

The female adam sinned by falling for the temptations and deception of the devil through the dragon or serpent, while the male adam sinned by coveting the beauty of the natural world and his wife's affection and companionship too irresistible. Both the male adam and the female adam saw the fruit from the Tree of the Knowledge of Good and Evil as a way of acquiring knowledge of good and evil independent of God, which became sin because they desired to see their own self as an idol, knowing good and evil like God.

Although Adam and Eve were created upright without sin (Ecclesiastes 7:29), this only meant that they were innocent but not perfect. To receive a perfect score, you must take and score perfect answers on a test. Until one takes and earns a perfect score on the test, one remains innocent but not perfect, because one's faith must be tested before you are perfect. Adam and Eve would have become perfect had Eve had a perfect score on her test by resisting the dragon's temptation and not eating the forbidden fruit. Adam would have had a perfect score on his test by obeying God and resisting the natural affection for his wife, Eve, and not eating the forbidden fruit. If Adam and Eve had earned a perfect score on their tests that God had for them, eventually God Intended to enter Adam and Eve as His resting abode or Temple (John 14: 15–17, 23).

If Adam and Eve had passed the test of not eating the fruit from the forbidden tree, God would conclude, "And it is good." However, the first female adam fell for the dragon's temptation and sinned against God's law and the first male Adam sinned by falling for the affection of his wife over the commandment of God. Being a just God He had to cancel His intimate relationship with Adam and Eve and had to dispel them from the Garden.

God had to wait until the appearance on earth of the Last Adam and Second Man, Christ Jesus, Who was born of a virgin woman, Who did not fall for the temptation of the devil in the wilderness, and Who qualified to bring redemption for fallen man and woman through His sacrificial death on the Roman Cross to those who accept Him as Redeemer, Lord, and Savior. Once that occurred God's seal of approval was placed on His chosen resting place or Temple.

Isaiah 66:1 announces God's supremacy: "Thus says the Lord, 'The heaven is My throne, and the earth is My footstool. Where is the house you will build for Me? Where is the place of My rest?'" Jesus became the Sabbath, the Seventh Day embodiment, the Godhead's Temple (Colossians 2:9). When Christ Jesus' Ekklesia was established, and after His death, resurrection, and ascension, the Ekklesia became God's Temple (1 Corinthians 3:16; 2 Corinthians 6:16; Ephesians 2:21), joined Christ Jesus as His Body, and became the place of God's Sabbath when and where God entered as His Resting Place. The Ekklesia shares God's Sabbath rest because the Godhead lives inside Believers.

Christ Jesus was given the privilege by the Father to pronounce the creative seal on the resting place of God upon His departure from earth, which was the body of Christ.

In Luke 10:21, Jesus proclaimed the crescendo of God's unwinding immanent plan which was to reconcile mankind to Himself to defeat the devil and reestablish His resting place when He said, "Even so, Father; for so it seemed good in Thy sight." In John 14:2,16-17, 23, Jesus makes it clear that His disciples will become the Resting Place: "In My Father's house are many mansions (mone)... I go to prepare a place for you. And if I go and prepare a place for you, I will come again, and receive you to Myself....And I will pray the Father, and he shall give you another Comforter, that He may abide with you forever (17)Even the Spirit of truth; whom the world cannot receive, because it seeth Him not, neither knoweth Him: but ye know Him; for He dwelleth with you, and shall be in you....(23) If a man loves Me, he will keep My words: and My Father will love him, and We (God the Father, Jesus divine nature God the Word, and God the Holy Spirit) will come unto him, and make Our (God the Father, Jesus divine nature God the Word, and God the Holy Spirit) abode (Greek-mone) with him." Interesting, the Greek word *mone* means a temporary dwelling place to stay while you are on your journey. Heaven is not Believers' final destination but back here on earth to rule and reign with Christ with new resurrected bodies for all eternity (Revelation Chapter 21; 1 Corinthians 15:23; Daniel 7:14, 17-22, 27; Revelation 5:10).

The same Greek word, mone, is used in both Scriptures to mean abode. When Jesus said, "I go to prepare a place for you," He meant that His suffering, death, resurrection, and ascension would be His work to prepare the mone, mansion, Temple, or resting place for God, which is the body of Christ. Wherever God lives, the place will become His Temple, His mansion, and His resting place because of His presence. Therefore, "in My Father's house are many mansions" because He now lives in a multi-people called Believers, corporately consisting of His Temple, with the ultimate destiny back here on earth where God lives inside Believers eternally (Revelation 21:3).

The fullness of the Godhead entered His rest by indwelling redeemed mankind, both man and woman, not just the man. Both men and women equally have been chosen as the Temple and resting place of God Who dwells in communion with the immortal male functioning born again spirits of Believers, man, and woman, individually and corporately. From His resting place and Temple, the Godhead will continue to do His work in and through Believers, man, and woman, while perfecting the immortal female functioning soul of each Believer subduing the mortal male functioning body until resurrection morning just as God made the new immortal male functioning born again spirit. The born-again spirit is perfect and incorruptible (1 Peter 1:23), which is holy and righteous (Ephesians 2:24) is the marital head of the immortal female functioning soul. So, the soul's response should be spiritually transformed to become spiritually mature. The final step in human-kind's perfection will be when Jesus returns to earth with Believers when Believers receive their perfect, sin-less, new creation resurrected male functioning bodies (1 Corinthians 15:23). The devil's diabolical plan was to steal the authority from the woman by deception, and from the man's temptation of affection knowing God's sense of justice required God to separate Himself from fallen man.

To accomplish his evil purpose the devil had to spoil God's plan but work within God's creative purpose of ordaining man as the under rulers of the earth; so, the devil surreptitiously would make the man and woman the devil's under rulers instead of God's under rulers and thereby usurping the first man and first woman's under ruler dominion authority.

The devil devised a plan to cause the innocent immortal male functioning spirit and the immortal female functioning soul to eat the forbidden fruit. This would be accomplished by deceiving the woman. Then with the woman's help the man would eat the forbidden fruit because of his affection for his wife was the tempta-tion and choice of the man.

If man and woman sinned, their fallen immortal male functioning spirits would no longer be functioning, so there would be no communion with God. God would remove His Temple out of the Garden of Eden and re-move the man and woman from the garden.

So, the diabolical scheme was the devil's plan to stop the functioning of the immortal male functioning spirit having the communion with God because God had to separate himself from fellowship with man as a form of death that was immediate and ongoing in both the man and woman after sin. The devil's plan also was to demote the immortal female functioning soul of both the man and woman to seek her stimuli nourishment only from the mortal male functioning body who every day was in the process of dying. The law of sin and death would be in operation after the fall.

The lie of the devil, even after the fall: The mortal male functioning body of both man and woman would not be granted the right to eat from the Tree of Life and become an immortal. The devil had only one member left in man that was immortal, and that was the female functioning soul; but the devil knew both man and woman immortal female functioning soul had a triune nature like God.

The first male adam and female adam wanted to be like God and became self-centered. The man and woman's immortal female functioning soul became an idol to be worshipped by man and woman as they became self-absorbed. They were not servants of others but concentrated on serving themselves.

Historically, the devil convinced the fallen immortal female functioning soul in both the man and woman there was no spiritual world, the physical world came about through evolution and not creation, there was no other god except self, that the only law was survival of the fittest, that money and possessions were the way to accumulate power, prestige, fame, and self-exaltation. The fallen immortal female functioning soul came to the belief in her heart that through the superior use of the mind, emotions, and heart, she could deceive many that she was superior to others and would use the attraction of the physical attributes of the male functioning body, her higher intelligence, the ability to act out emotions, and the superior fallen beliefs in false religions was the pathway to rich a and famous lifestyle. When the fallen immortal female functioning soul deems herself as rich and famous, then she can join the higher class of the social and political elitest, where the competition to stay on top is ferocious and often a cause of early death.

The attractiveness of the ego boosting idol of elitism causes both fallen man and woman to seek what only a very few achieve. Yet, it is very costly to maintain the status as the rich and famous elites because it requires the man and woman not to be conservative in the use of their money, as they must continue to spin buying expensive houses, cars, clothes, restaurants, vacations, and often end up with divorce. When rich and famous die, they want everyone to know they died rich and famous because they want people to remember them after death. Unfortunately, the dead fallen man and woman's memory is generally gone after one or two generations at best.

As a fallen man and woman elitest, unlike other men and women who do not want to achieve that status, the fallen immortal female functioning soul of both man and woman have this enate desire to take dominion over their profession, business, or political office for recognition and acquisition of a continuous flow of money.

The fallen ruler of this world, Lucifer, Satan, the devil, teaches through his established false religion that existence here on earth in this life is for self-gratification, self-focused, self-exaltation, self-aggrandizement, self-actualization, self-motivation, self-centeredness, self-focused, and self-rulership over others.

Unfortunately, for the fallen man and woman, this is how the king of the kingdom of darkness controls his select few elitists who he helped become rich and famous; and now they owe him their allegiance and lives.

The devil does not care if these elitists do not worship him, so long as they do not worship God Almighty. The devil wants these elitists to be false idols to snare other fallen men and women in his trap to pursue to be rich and famous. If these elitists worship themselves that is okay with the devil.

The devil uses his special fallen rich and famous leaders in human form by putting them sometimes in government and in every other profession, sports, entertainment, and industry where the acquisition of fame and riches justify their place of authority, presumed mental or physical superiority, and as the chosen elite ones.

There are a few super wealthy financiers who the devil causes them to fund the election of certain strategic local, state Prosecutors, state Legislatures, Governors, and federal Senators, House Representatives, Presidents, or other politicians to advance the cause of the devil and his kingdom of darkness and specifically to attack opposing people running for office that the devil does not want in government office. The devil causes some super wealthy financiers to purchase ownership in news media outlets and social internet channels to control the narrative and topics of interest. Unfortunately, many falshoods are presented through mass media which makes the falsehoods the new norm.

Although God is longsuffering, there is always a day of death and judgment for all men and women. Every man and woman face either eternal life or infernal death. Only God knows the day and hour of death, so, every fallen man and woman must accept Jesus Christ as Lord and Savior to avoid an everlasting infernal Lake of Fire. If they are thrown into the Lake of Fire for all eternity, the pain and suffering is unimaginable. Thus, the question to consider is whether the pursuit of fame and fortune on condition they stay unsaved worth the future afterlife misery?

The devil was convinced that he had won in spoiling God's plan for dominion of the earth through the man by the success of the devil's plan to deceive the woman, hoping the man would choose the affections of the woman over the commandment of God, and the devil's planned works.

The devil knew that God's divine justice would demand God's divine judgment of death and separation from the man and woman when the man and woman disobeyed, where separation from communion with God is the form of death of immortal beings. In a sense the devil was correct.

Yet, hidden in the bosom of God was God's only begotten Son with a humanity nature that was already born of God, and whose divine nature was God the Word. God's only begotten Son was born, but not created, before the first earthy man and woman and the devil were created. God spoke His judgment against the devil that the Seed of the woman would crush the "headship authority" of the seed of the serpent/dragon in Genesis 3:15. The devil knew that the woman did not create a Seed, but rather an egg; so, the devil knew that sometime in the future that God had a plan to bring in a Redeemer, a Messiah, a Son King to rule the earth born of a virgin that would bring God's Kingdom back to earth by a sinless man once again.

At first, the devil's plan was to spread as much evil in the world and in man to potentially make God want to destroy mankind and start over by creating a new Creature. In the meantime, the devil usurped man's authority in the earth. Thus, Genesis says that there were giants called Nephilim in the time of great evil in the land; and there were great spiritual beings called rebellious sons of God entering the daughters of Adam and Eve who gave birth to the gibbor that became mighty men of renown (Genesis 6:4-8). Jude 1:6 says, "And the angels which kept not their first estate, but left their own habitation, He hath reserved in everlasting chains under darkness unto the judgment of the great day."

The devil's deception and diabolical plan did not catch God off guard, as God is all knowing and knew what was going to happen because God is not restricted by time as the devil is. God knew that Adam and Eve were going to sin.

The devil had to operate through the body of the serpent/dragon to appear to the woman since the devil had no body himself. To exercise rulership over the earth, the devil had to entice those who were granted rulership authority by God, i.e., the man and woman. Today, demons are disembodied spirits who trespass humans' bodies and animal bodies to exercise possessory authority. Demons are not allowed to forcibly achieve this act toward humans; so, they must come in through a door left open by fallen man's negligence or through a door in mankind opened by deception, trespass, betrayal, physical, psychological abuse, drugs, alcohol, or sin.

Accordingly, the devil's plan in convincing the first woman, who in turn entice the first man to fall into sin was for the purpose of usurping the man and woman's under-rulership authority ordained by God to them to take dominion over the earth. God still owned the earth (Psalm 24:1), but the result of the fall was that man's possessory authority was unlawfully usurped and used by the devil and his kingdom of darkness over the sons of disobedience (Ephesians 2:1-3).

The devil's dragon: Genesis 3:1-2 is the conversation between the woman and the serpent/dragon that began the actual downfall of all mankind. "Now the serpent was more subtle than any beast of the field which the LORD God had made. And he said unto the woman, Yea, hath God said, 'Ye shall not eat of every tree of the garden?"

The Hebrew word for serpent is nawkhawsh, and is pronounced naw-khawsh; and is derived from the root word nawkhash. Nawkhawsh is translated as enchant and divine in several places in the Scriptures (Genesis 44:15, Leviticus 19:26, Deuteronomy 18:10, 2 Chronicles 33:6). The Hebrew word nawkhash means to hiss, that is, whisper a spell; to prognosticate, divine, enchanter, and to learn by experience, indeed, diligently observe as opposed to divine wisdom and knowledge from God.

For example, Leviticus 19:26 says, "Ye shall not eat anything with the blood: neither shall ye use enchantment (Hebrew-nawkhash), nor observe times (Hebrew anan meaning magic)."

When Moses met God at the burning bush, God told Moses in Exodus 4:3 to use his staff which he had used for years "And He (God) said, 'Cast it on the ground. And he cast it on the ground, and it became a serpent (Hebrew nawkhawsh, enchanter which appeared as a dragon); and Moses fled from before it." Moses encountered many natural serpents and killed them while leading Jethro's sheep for forty years, so why did he run from this particular serpent? Or was it really a dragon?

Look what Moses' same staff became later before Pharoah. Moses came back to Egypt, and God instructed Moses and Aaron in Exodus 7:9 and said, "When Pharaoh shall speak unto you, saying, 'Shew a miracle for you:' then thou shalt say unto Aaron, 'Take thy rod, and cast it before Pharoah, and it shall become a serpent (Hebrew tannîyn pronounced tan neen)." This Hebrew word tannîyn means dragon, not serpent; so, the same staff that was used to bring forth in front of Pharoah a dragon was called a serpent or enchanter when the same staff was thrown to the ground.

Finally, Revelation 20:2 says, "And he (Angel) laid hold on the dragon, that old serpent, which is the devil, and Satan, and bound him a thousand years." Genesis 3:1 says, "Now the serpent was more subtle than any other beast in the field...." The word subtle is the Hebrew word arum, which means cunning, crafty, prudent, subtle, smooth, or walks with a certain subtle gate. The dragon was used by the devil to do his deceptive conversation with the first woman. The dragon was referred to as the Old Serpent.

Matthew 16: 21-23 says, "From that time forth began Jesus to shew unto His disciples, how that He must go unto Jerusalem, and suffer many things of the elders and chief priests and scribes, and be killed, and be raised again the third day. (22) Then Peter took Him, and began to rebuke Him, saying, 'Be it far from thee, Lord: this shall not be unto thee. (23) But He turned, and said unto Peter, 'Get thee behind me, Satan: thou art an offence unto me: for thou savourest not the things that be of God, but those that be of men.'"

The conversation between the dragon and the first woman. Genesis 3:2–3 says, "And the woman said unto the serpent, 'We may eat of the fruit of the trees of the garden: (3) But of the fruit of the tree, which is in the midst of the garden, God hath said, 'Ye shall not eat of it, neither shall ye touch it, lest ye die.'"

The conversation between the first woman and the serpent (better dragon) began the original sin and actual downfall of all mankind. The woman added to God's Word as God had not forbidden man to touch the banned fruit, but only not to eat it. If the woman was repeating what the first man had said, then the man had added to God's word when he instructed the first woman while he should have taught her God's commandment with strict accuracy. Likewise, the woman was weakening the certainty of God's death sentence when she said, "lest you die." The woman's watered-down words of "lest you die" took away the full effect of immediate dying or "surely die" after breaking God's word, commandment, law, and will.

Genesis 3:4-5, 7 reveals the serpent's craftiness: "And the serpent said unto the woman, 'Ye shall not surely die: For God doth know that in the day ye eat thereof, then your eyes shall be opened, and ye shall be as gods, knowing good and evil.'... And the eyes of them both were opened, and they knew that they were naked; and they sewed fig leaves together and made themselves aprons.'"

Romans 5:12 says, "Wherefore, as by one man sin entered into the world, and death by sin; and so, death passed upon all men, for that all have sinned." When the first woman and man sinned, their immortal male functioning spirits immediately entered a state of spiritual death, sleep, or coma, although the first man and woman's immortal female functioning souls and mortal male functioning bodies were still alive and functioning. Spiritual death entered the world at that point and spread to all of Adam and Eve's offspring and posterity. The sin of the immortal male functioning spirit of both the man and woman destroyed the union the immortal male functioning spirit had with God and a state of sleep, or a coma permanently came in their immortal male functioning spirits. Their immortal male functioning spirits would never be resurrected. Isaiah 59:2 says, "But your iniquities have separated between you and your God, and your sins have hid His face from you, that he will not hear."

Since the male functioning body was mortal, he was destined to die anyway unless he had eaten the fruit from the Tree of Life; so, the death that is being referred to is the death of the first man and first woman's immortal male functioning spirit. The appearance of life after sin added to the devil's descent, but the first man's eating the forbidden fruit became Adam's high treason, for God had personally commanded not to eat the fruit from the forbidden tree.

Redeemed man and woman by Christ Jesus had to become new creatures in Christ with new immortal male functioning born again spirits (2 Corinthians 5:17). Romans 5:16-19 says, "And not as it was by one that sinned, so, is the gift: for the judgment was by one to condemnation, but the free gift is of many offences unto justification. (17) For if by one man's offence death reigned by one; much more they which receive abundance of grace and of the gift of righteousness shall reign in life by one, Jesus Christ.) (18) Therefore, as by the offence of one judgment came upon all men to condemnation; even so by the righteousness of one the free gift came upon all men unto justification of life. (19) For as by one man's disobedience many were made sinners, so by the obedience of one shall many be made righteous."

The word "eyes" in Genesis 3:7 were referring to eyes of the first man and first woman's immortal female functioning souls, which before were seeing information brought to her by the sinless immortal male functioning spirit and the sinless mortal male functioning body, which at that time were still doing Godly good fulfilling their Godly purposes.

Godly good is different than the self-centered fallen good contained in the Tree of the Knowledge of Good and Evil. Before the fall, the presence of God's glory light enveloped Adam and Eve, and their soulish eyes perceived the spiritual glory God put on His created things.

In fact, before the fall, Adam and Eve's immortal female functioning soulish eyes perceived their mortal male functioning bodies clothed in God's glory light; and their immortal male functioning spirits before the fall saw into the spiritual realm the beauty of and glory light on God's natural creation. After the fall, their soulish eyes were opened to perceived information from the physical world unclothed without their created glory light from God that protected their innocence. Thus, they knew that after they had sinned, they were naked.

Since the devil knew that the first man had failed as a teacher and marital head, the first woman, although sinless but innocent, could be deceived because her weakness was the lack of accurate Godly instruction from the first man. Additionally, the first woman craved after self-knowledge in her immortal female functioning soul and who desired to be an independent person. The crafty devil, speaking through the dragon, knew that her immortal female functioning soul was secretly coveting a desire to know things outside of God; so, her will could be manipulated if it could get her to think she would be fulfilling her secret desire by eating the forbidden fruit of the knowledge of good and evil.

Thus, the devil planned his deception through the dragon to deceive the immortal female functioning soul of the woman to know things independently of God. This was Satan's second reason for having the serpent to say in Genesis 3:5 that "For God knows that in the day you eat of it your (soulish) eyes will be opened, and you will be like God knowing good and evil." The serpent lied, as the experience was not the source of such fallen and forbidden knowledge. Without being warned of the theft that was about to occur, Eve's rebellion in eating the fruit from the Tree of the Knowledge of Good and Evil caused usurpation of Eve's (and Adam's) authority to rule here on earth, and the dominion authority was transferred by default to Satan and his kingdom of darkness.

This earthly, self-centered knowledge of good and evil was forbidden by God, for this was Satan's fallen, perverted wisdom (James 3:15) and the very thing that caused Lucifer to commit sin and fall from his high position as the Morning Star and the Cherub that covered the throne of God (Isaiah 14:12-14; Ezekiel 28:11-19).

The forbidden fruit from the Tree of the Knowledge of Good and Evil: Eve wanted to make herself an idol, a god, independently knowing good and evil like Creator God.

Eve desired earthly knowledge of what was good for her self-centeredness and self-exaltation to obtain self-rule through independent humanistic sensory knowledge and four-dimensional deductive reasoning, as opposed to God's rule through dependency on God's higher divine illumination through God's revelation, inspiration, and wisdom that comes from submission and obedience to Him. The woman lost her trust in God and His word and accepted the lie of Satan speaking through the dragon; so, her doubt in God's word turned into unbelief in her heart (1 Timothy 2:13-15).

Again, the good from the Tree of the Knowledge of Good and Evil does not mean God's divine good. This was perverted, selfish good, good that enhances self-image, which was Humanism; whereas, God's knowledge and wisdom of His good was designed to enhance the woman as the image of God, not making herself a god. Eve thought the good from the Tree of the Knowledge of Good and Evil was what showed good taste, good looks, and good image as an independent entity apart from God.

All three kinds of temptations that led to sins were committed by the woman and then the man (1 John 2:15-17). Genesis 3:6-7 says, "So, when the woman saw that the tree was good for food (lust of the flesh), that it was pleasant to the eyes (lust of the eyes), and a tree desirable to make one wise (pride of life), she took of its fruit and ate. She also gave it to her husband with her, and he ate it. Then the eyes of both were opened, and they knew that they were naked...."

The man and woman's immortal female functioning souls exercised their wills to reject the love and immortal life of God in exchange for the deceptive fulfillment of depraved sensory knowledge from the natural world, which resulted in infernal death and decay, unless redeemed by God's acceptable Savior.

Let us examine a little closer this forbidden fruit containing good and evil.

The Tree of the Knowledge of Good and Evil was not the Tree of the Knowledge of Right and Wrong. Adam knew what was right and wrong, as God had told him not to eat the forbidden fruit. Right was and is doing what God commands to do or not doing what God forbids doing. Wrong is doing what God commands not to do or not doing what God says to do. Besides, this tree was not the Tree of the Knowledge of Experience. When Adam and Eve disobeyed God, were they through their disobedience to experience a more complete knowledge of Godly good? It is easy to understand that their disobedience resulted in knowing evil. Can one receive the knowledge of good from a disobedient act? What good can come from disobeying God? Obviously, none!

The principle is that the knowledge of good and evil does not come through experience of the five senses. Knowledge of good and evil comes from the spiritual world because the design, nature, and purpose of all things created came from the spiritual world. Hence, self-centered good and evil came from Satan's spiritual kingdom of darkness.

God said in Genesis 3:22 that: "...Behold the man (generic reference to man as both male and female) has become as one of Us, to know good and evil ...." If knowledge of good and evil had its roots from experiential knowledge, then God would have had to experience sin, violate God's own principles, and entertain temptation to know evil.

God never sinned, never violated His own principles, nor could be tempted to commit evil or sin; so, knowledge of good and evil does not need to come from experience (James 1:13). God never made anything with both good and evil in it, except the Tree of Knowledge of Good and Evil. This tree was made with the good and evil of self-centered knowledge brought into the Garden of Eden from the spiritual realm because of Lucifer's rebellion against God. God said in the creation verses of Genesis that the things He created were inherently good when fulfilling His purposes and were not created with self centered good and self-centered evil residing in and manifesting through them.

Everything that God created was made to serve other created things, like animals, birds, fishes, and people. Fruit trees, vegetable plants, lions, tigers, monkeys, wolves, cows, horses, chickens, ducks, dogs, cats, and humans were not designed to eat their own kind. Vegetables do not eat their produce vegetables and fruit trees do not eat their own fruit. Angels were designed to minister to the heirs of salvation, and people were designed to be servants of other people.

Lucifer or the devil was the true source of evil. Jesus said in John 8:44, "Ye are of your father the devil, and the lusts of your father ye will do. He was a murderer from the beginning, and abode not in the truth, because there is no truth in him. When he speaketh a lie, he speaketh of his own: for he is a liar, and the father of it."

Evil originally came from the influence and actions of a fallen being, named Lucifer, who additionally means morning star, son of the dawn, shining one, light-bearer, angel of light, Satan, devil, prince of the power of the air, the god of this world, the ruler of this world, slanderer, Beelzebub, a roaring lion roaming the earth seeing whom he may desire, an angel of light, the dragon, and the serpent. Isaiah 14:12 says, "How art thou fallen from heaven, O Lucifer, son of the morning! How art thou cut down to the ground, which didst weaken the nations!" In Isaiah 14:12 the Hebrew from the King James translation of Lucifer is Heylel, which means, again, morning star, son of the dawn, shining one, or light bearer, but also means to shine, hence, to make a show of self, a boasting, proud, rave about yourself, self-praise, to be renown.

Lucifer was called the morning star, son of the dawn, shining one, or light bearer; and he speaking through the dragon brought deception in the Garden to tempt the female adam to eat the forbidden fruit; and he then caused the female adam to tempt the male adam to commit high treason against God by eating the forbidden fruit because God commanded the male adam not to do it. As a result, the whole world fell under the spell of this wicked, very powerful spiritual being and his kingdom of darkness.

Thus, fallen good and fallen evil did not really originate from the male adam and female adam's experience of eating the forbidden fruit, but from the spiritual world of darkness. Disobedience of the commandment of the highest infinite Creator Spirit, Almighty God, was just opening the doorway into the kingdom of darkness. Knowing good and evil was a fallen state of existence for mankind because mankind entered a relationship with the devil and gave up their intimate relationship with God. All knowledge comes from that imparted through intimacy in relationship (Hosea 4:6).

After man's fall, God's sovereign, holy, just, and righteous principles caused Him to stop His intimate relationship with mankind, and man had to live in a world governed by a new dark prince who is evil personified. The devil's desire is for fallen mankind to have intimacy with him or with God's natural world, which becomes idol worship. The evil intimacy is true of the wrongful attachment to money. 1 Timothy 6:10 says, "For the love of money is the root of all evil: which while some coveted after, they have erred from the faith, and pierced themselves through with many sorrows." The wrongful attachment to money reveals that it is not money that is the root of all kinds of evil but the love or worship of it. It is the unlawful relationship with the created thing or person that is the sin. Idol worship of money is sin, but worse, the idol worship is opening the doorway into the kingdom of darkness that becomes the root of all kinds of evil. Idol worship is the worse kind of sin, as it violates the first and second commandments.

In 1 Corinthians 2:14, Paul said, "But the natural man does not receive the things of the Spirit of God, for they are foolishness to him; nor can he know them, because they are spiritually discerned." The word natural is the Greek word psuchikos, which means soulishly led or controlled by the influence of the sensory knowledge from the mortal male functioning body, physical world, spiritual rebellious knowledge from cult teaching or from the kingdom of darkness through demons.

In today's time, without the new immortal male functioning born again spirit, the immortal female functioning soul cannot readily receive spiritual truth, wisdom, knowledge, and understanding from God, even by studying the logos word, a true prophet, or someone with the gift of a word of knowledge. The reason is Godly spiritual truth, wisdom, knowledge, and understanding can be discerned if the person becomes a Believer, receives an immortal male functioning born again spirit from Christ Jesus, and submits and enters into an intimate relationship with God and the Lord.

Like priming a pump with water, new Believers need Ministers who function as apostles, prophets, evangelist, pastors, or teachers "For the perfecting of the saints, for the work of the ministry, for the edifying of the body of Christ" (Ephesians 4:11-12). New Believers need to study the Bible habitually and be able to discern what is spiritual from the Holy Spirit and the Kingdom of God rather than of the fallen world or the kingdom of darkness. The Bible is a lens through which Believers need to discern truth, righteousness, peace, and joy in the Holy Spirit, seeking first the Kingdom of God as opposed to the fallen world or the Kingdom of darkness.

After salvation, the Godhead, Himself, participates in the transformation of the Believer's immortal female functioning soul after initial salvation. On the other hand, before salvation, the immortal female functioning soul is subject to the unclean, unhealthy, and deceptive demonic spirits that are male in function as they bring evil stimuli to tempt the fallen immortal female functioning mind, emotions, and heart in the soul. Demonic forces work by tempting the flesh to sin, but the body needs the soul to agree to exercise the will to sin.

Why must the immortal female functioning soul need spiritual transformation? Even after being born again, soulish sin opens the door of the law of sin and death, which leads even the Believer down the path of evil in the fallen world and the kingdom of darkness that activates the consequences of the law of sowing and reaping (Galatians 6:7-8). The immortal female functioning soul is the recipient of knowledge into the mind, the recipient of feelings into the emotions, and the recipient of beliefs into the heart to effectuate a decision with the will. To contravene the man and woman Believer is encouraged to seek first the Kingdom of God and His righteousness every day, every hour, while in prayer, while at work, while in school, and every other place and activity. Believers are to make seeking the Kingdom of God and His righteousness a lifestyle, not something to do on their days off from work or a particular spiritual holiday.

1 Peter 3:7 says in relevant part that: "Husbands, likewise, dwell with them (wives) with understanding...." The same rule applies to the relationship between the immortal male functioning born again spirit who must dwell with the immortal female functioning soul with understanding.

The immortal male functioning born again spirit and mortal male functioning body are in competition to obtain the attention of the immortal female functioning soul. The immortal male functioning born again spirit gathers spiritual stimuli from the Kingdom of God to convince the immortal female functioning soul to submit to God's transformation discipline and to receive the forgiveness, love, truth, and life from God. On the other hand, even after salvation, the mortal male functioning body gathers natural sinful stimuli in the world to obtain the attention of the immortal female functioning soul and tries to convince the non-transformed mind, emotions, and heart that transformation of the immortal female functioning soul is optional and not necessary to be saved, as salvation is a gift and not works (Ephesians 2:8-9). Yet, the soul needs to be transformed after initial salvation.

1 Corinthians 3:11-19 says, "For other foundation can no man lay than that is laid, which is Jesus Christ. (12) Now if any man builds upon this foundation gold, silver, precious stones, wood, hay, stubble; (13) every man's work shall be made manifest: for the day shall declare it, because it shall be revealed by fire; and the fire shall try every man's work of what sort it is. (14) If any man's work abides which he hath built thereupon, he shall receive a reward. (15) If any man's work shall be burned, he shall suffer loss: but he himself shall be saved; yet so as by fire. (16) Know ye not that ye are the temple of God, and that the Spirit of God dwelleth in you? (17) If any man defiles the temple of God, him shall God destroy; for the temple of God is holy, which temple ye are. (18) Let no man deceive himself. If any man among you seemeth to be wise in this world, let him become a fool, that he may be wise. (19) For the wisdom of this world is foolishness with God. For it is written, He taketh the wise in their own craftiness."

The immortal male functioning born again spirit competes with the mortal male functioning body for the attention of the immortal female functioning soul.

Galatians 5:16-18 says, "This I say then, 'Walk in the Spirit, and ye shall not fulfill the lust of the flesh. (17) For the flesh lusteth against the (immortal male functioning born again) spirit, and the (immortal male functioning born again) spirit against the flesh: and these are contrary the one to the other: so that ye cannot do the things that ye would.'"

The immortal female functioning soul eventually sees no betterment in her life by accepting fleshly stimuli from the world that is the only thing that the mortal male functioning body has to offer, for the immortal female functioning soul knows that the mortal male functioning body is dying and has no spiritual discernment. The immortal female functioning soul understands she will live on as an immortal being after the mortal male functioning body dies and decays back to dust, but hopes for a new creation body like Jesus when Jesus returns (1 Corinthians 15:23; Revelation Chapter 21).

God first pursues the immortal female functioning soul and makes her unsatisfied with her mere existence in this fallen world. In response, the immortal female functioning soul invites God and His Christ in her mind, emotions, and heart. Jesus said in John 6:44 "No man can come to Me, except the Father which hath sent Me draw him: and I will raise him up at the last day."

The immortal female functioning soul sees the mortal male functioning body continuously getting older and heading for death. The immortal female functioning soul ponders about an afterlife and wants to know and obtain the way, truth, and life. Discerning there is evidence of a desire for the way, truth, and life, God comes to the immortal female functioning soul usually through a trusted friend Believer or through a Minister that preaches the gospel of the Kingdom and preaches the message of repentance and remission of sins that lead to life everlasting with Christ Jesus in the Kingdom of God. It is the female part of both man and woman that receives God's loving goodness and receives the steps for man to be saved by calling on the name of the Lord Jesus for salvation (Romans 10:13). Jesus said in John 6:63, "... the flesh profiteth nothing...." The immortal female functioning soul hears the gospel message of God's wonderful Kingdom and salvation and that it is the goodness of God that leads to repentance (Romans 2:4).

Thus, the female part of man and women should receive gratitude and thanks for responding to the call of Father God to come to Jesus, the Kingdom of God, repent, receive remission of sins, and receive the gift of eternal salvation based upon Jesus' sacrifice of His life on the Roman Cross. Romans 10:13 says, "For whosoever shall call upon the name of the Lord shall be saved."

The immortal female functioning soul receives illumination that God has a different goodness than the Tree of the Knowledge of good and evil. God's goodness is eternal, so the immortal female functioning soul rejects the devil, the fallen world, and the flesh's definition of goodness. Before initial salvation, the immortal female functioning soul comes to the resolve in response to God's urging that the good that came from the forbidden fruit is only good for self-promotion, idol worship of self, constitutes rebellion against God, and leads to infernal death.

The immortal female functioning soul then makes the mortal male function body confess with his mouth the Lord Jesus, and the immortal female functioning soul believes in her heart that God raised Jesus from the dead (Romans 10:9). The immortal female functioning soul immediately receives salvation and has the gift of everlasting life to live with the Godhead and Christ Jesus' humanity nature forever in the Kingdom of God. Yet, the immortal female functioning soul understands she still has her old thoughts, remembrance of emotional outbursts, and a heart that still has some competing wrong beliefs. She seeks the Holy Spirit, "What must I do to get rid of these sinful, unhealthy thoughts, feelings, and beliefs?" Sometimes, the saved immortal female functioning soul is stubborn and is not willing to undergo humility training, studying the word of God, becoming spiritual and no longer carnal, and confronting her past hurts, failures, and memories of betrayals, as they have become part of her personality and historical life experiences. The secret is to not just reject your past hurts, trespasses, sins, or failures, but to confront them, take charge over them. This causes you to gain bravery instead of victimization.

What the immortal female functioning soul did not know or did not understand that suddenly upon receiving initial salvation and eternal life that a new companion is present within her who is the perfect, sinless, righteous, and holy immortal male functioning born again spirit, who with the leading of the Holy Spirit will come into the immortal female functioning soul, bringing righteousness, peace, joy, holiness, and God's goodness. Likewise, the immortal female functioning soul discerns the presence of the Godhead as the male functioning body has become God's temple.

Righteousness, peace, joy, holiness, and God's goodness fills the immortal female functioning soul. Then, this new immortal male functioning born again spirit, along with the Holy Spirit visits the heart and starts establishing a new foundation of beliefs in line with Christ Jesus and the Kingdom of God. The immortal female functioning soul accepts as true that the Godhead now lives inside the mortal male functioning body as the Godhead's Temple, along with the new immortal male functioning born again spirit. The Godhead has asked permission to start the transformation of the immortal female functioning soul by spiritually renewing the mind (Romans 12:2), spiritually stabilizing the emotions (Isaiah 33:6), and establishing a new library of godly and kingdom beliefs in the heart (John 14:1).

Why does the Holy Spirit and immortal male functioning born again spirit go first to the heart in the immortal female functioning soul where the will resides instead of the mind or emotions? The reason is that neither the Holy Spirit nor the immortal male functioning born again spirit will trespass the will in the heart but waits until invited. The heart is where the action of sin manifests because that is where the will is, and the heart is where most of the evil is which continues to defile the mind and emotions of the immortal female functioning soul. Thus, by changing the beliefs in the heart in line with God and His word, the heart activates the will to act as the Lord's disciple and as a member of Father God's family by adoption (Romans

8:15).

Jesus said in Matthew 15:18-19, "But those things (especially beliefs) which proceed out of the mouth come forth from the heart; and they defile the man. (19) For out of the heart proceed evil thoughts, murders, adulteries, fornications, thefts, false witness, blasphemies." Only God can change the heart to bring forth righteousness, peace, joy, goodness, agape love, and spiritual beliefs. The immortal female functioning soul must want and request to be clean and have a new heart and must submit to God's reconstruction and transformation, starting with a new heart."

The Bible emphasizes that unbelievers do evil things because their hearts are evil, and since Believers' immortal female functioning souls were not born again as was the immortal male functioning born again spirit, then the immortal female functioning soul must respond to God for a clean heart (John 6:44). King David cried out in Psalms 51:10-13, "Create in me a clean heart, O God; and renew a right spirit within me. (11) Cast me not away from thy presence; and take not thy Holy Spirit from me. (12) Restore unto me the joy of thy salvation; and uphold me with thy free (born again) spirit. (13) Then will I teach transgressors thy ways; and sinners shall be converted unto thee."

The immortal female functioning soul discovered that she is now Christ Jesus' Betrothed and, in the future, she will be marrying Christ Jesus as His Bride; and she is informed that Jesus wants the immortal female functioning soul to not seek the sins of the flesh anymore but rather seek first the Kingdom of God and His righteousness. In so doing, the immortal female functioning soul will be part of a glorious church, not having spot, or wrinkle, or any such thing; but that she should be holy and without blemish (Ephesians 5:27).

In the meantime, the immortal female functioning soul is encouraged by the Holy Spirit that she is to have intimate fellowship with the New Man (immortal male functioning born again spirit) now present that is sinless, righteous, and holy (1 John 3:9; Ephesians 4:24). Additionally, the immortal female functioning soul is told that the entire Godhead is living with her, using the mortal male functioning body as their holy Temple; and there will be a divine re-construction crew that is going to completely transform and renovate the immortal female functioning soulish mind, emotions, and heart.

God the Father is going to prune away the flesh in the mind, emotions, and heart, so that they will produce the fruit of the Spirit (John 15:2). God the Word will wash away the dirt of the flesh and sanctify the mind, emotions, and heart with the water of the rhema word (Ephesians 5:26). God the Holy Spirit will mortify the deeds of the flesh in the mind, emotions, and heart to bring the riches of zoe life into the mind, emotions, and heart (Romans 8:13). The Holy Spirit tells the immortal female functioning soul that she is now in training for servanthood as a citizen of heaven (Philippians 3:20), Christ's Kingdom Ambassador (2 Corinthians 5:20), Christ's Kingdom Soldier (2 Timothy 2:3-4), a worshipper of God, and a Minister of God's word and Spirit.

The immortal female functioning soul was originally created by God to live protected inside and was not created to leave the mortal male functioning body until the mortal male functioning body dies. The immortal female functioning soul can only receive sensory and physical stimuli through the mortal male functioning body or spiritual and inspirational stimuli through the immortal male functioning born again spirit. The immortal female functioning soul uses the stimuli to imagine, ascertain, discover God laws, deduce conclusions from spiritual or natural knowledge, excite spiritual or natural feelings, and accept spiritual or natural beliefs. Unless these spiritual or natural stimuli are sent from the immortal male functioning born again spirit or mortal male functioning body, the immortal female functioning soul has no ability to acquire such knowledge, feelings, or beliefs, unless they come from a demon. Can a Believer have the influence of a demon? Wrong question. The correct question is, "Who wants a demon?" The second question is, "How do I get rid of the demon?"

The created male functions of both the man and woman strengthened them to interact publicly with other humans, and things in the spiritual and physical realities from which the male functions were created, made, formed, built, and assigned with the duty and task to gather, perceive, comprehend, understand, feel, observe, examine, and then transmit this spiritual stimuli and natural stimuli to the immortal female functioning soul to activate the will.

The stimuli brought by the immortal male functioning spirit before the fall of the male adam and female adam was made from the substance of the spiritual world; whereas the stimuli brought by the mortal male functioning body was made from the substance of the physical natural world. The immortal male functioning spirit was able to interact with other spiritual beings, including God, and things or entities in the spiritual world. The mortal male functioning body was restricted to the earth and all its natural life and surroundings. The mortal male functioning body does not understand spiritual things, but it knows that he is a Temple and spiritual beings live inside with the immortal female functioning soul.

After being born again through Christ Jesus, the indwelling Godhead in Believers guard the new immortal male functioning born again spirit from the attacks of evil spirits or the temptations of the flesh. The new immortal male functioning born again spirit as the New Man is perfect (Hebrews 12:23), is holy and righteous in the image of Christ (Ephesians 4:24; Colossians 3:10), and does not sin (1 John 3:9). Romans 2:29 says, "But he is a Jew, which is one inwardly; and circumcision is that of the heart, in the spirit, and not in the letter; whose praise is not of men, but of God."

The immortal female functioning soul craves spiritual knowledge, images, imaginative ideas, feelings, sounds of music, voices, things of beauty, and things and events that enhance the immortal female functioning soul's self-interest, prestige, and image. For example, men and women, especially women, spend lots of time with the right make-up, the right hairstyle, and the right clothes that enhances his or her prestige, and image. Most men and women Believers still spend lots of time in front of a mirror. Prestige and image is why the immature, untransformed immortal female functioning soul directs the mortal male functioning body to stand in front of a mirror; and she makes the mortal male functioning body have a beautiful or handsome look. Yet, how a Believer looks on her or his mortal male functioning body does not communicate the maturity or lack of maturity of the immortal female functioning soul. The immortal female functioning soul at first develops an image internally by the look of her mortal male functioning body.

The immortal female functioning soul develops an image and taste of what attracts her to the mortal male functioning body of another person with whom she can live and interact on a friendly and loving basis. God desires the immortal female functioning soul to have an intimate relationship with Him as He has with the immortal male functioning born again spirit, and God wants the immortal female functioning soul to choose a spouse based upon the spouse's spiritual maturity of his or her soul, not the beauty or handsomeness of the spouse's mortal functioning male body. Eventually the mortal male functioning body grows old and is no longer handsome or beautiful, so if the spouses do not see the spiritual beauty of the immortal female functioning soul, then there can develop a dislike of the other spouse and trust and love wanes.

After the fall of the male adam and the female adam, what seemed good to the senses of the mortal male functioning body became acceptable common sense for the immortal female functioning soul living together while the spirit was in a coma sleep or "dead in sins" (Ephesians 2:1). This common sense became the best the mortal male functioning body with the five senses living in the physical world could offer to the immortal female functioning soul; so, the mortal male functioning body tried to dominate the subjects of communication by feeding the immortal female functioning soul with natural stimuli the mortal male functioning body wanted the immortal female functioning soul to activate the will to satisfy the mortal male functioning body's lustful needs. Good and evil were relegated to being defined as to what seemed to be good or evil in the natural physical world to the immortal female functioning soul and the mortal male functioning body living and interacting together without the old immortal male functioning spirit.

When the male adam and the female adam sinned, their immortal male functioning spirits inside of them immediately became non-functioning; and their mortal male functioning bodies relegated to interacting in the world started to rule over their immortal female functioning souls who were created to live inside. Yet, the fall of man and woman caused an unnatural relationship between the immortal female functioning soul and the mortal male functioning body. This became a contest of the immortal female functioning soul trying to convince the mortal male functioning body to do things that stimulated the immortal female functioning soul's needs, as opposed to the mortal male functioning body's deeds of the flesh. Today, the immortal female functioning soul likes to go to concerts, movies, art galleries, sports events, walks on the beach to hear the ocean waves, or go out to a romantic dinner with another immortal female functioning soul mate. So, the immortal female functioning soul sends the mortal male functioning body to the beauty parlor, gets nails polished, hair styled, and make-up and puts on stylish clothes. The immortal female functioning soul causes the mortal male functioning body to speak positive witty things to make the interaction with the friend pleasant and memorable.

After the fall, man and woman's dominion mandate granted by God in Genesis 1:26-28 became perverted; and man and woman's fallen immortal female functioning souls and fallen mortal male functioning bodies lived in sin and started trying to take dominion over other humans. Man and woman started worshipping self, which was forbidden by God. God forbade man and woman from trying to take dominion over other men and women. As a result, fights, murders, thefts, hatreds, competitions, confusion, strife, jealousies, divisions, arguments, defamations of character, suspicions, lust of the flesh, lust of the eyes, pride of life, egocentric selfishness, avarice, greed, covetousness, and all other kinds of sins often became the norm in relationships between fallen mankind.

Wrongful Dominion: Wars started, kingdoms, against kingdoms, forcibly taking another King's lands, redefining when life begins resulting in genocide in the womb, enslavements based upon race or historical origin, genocide of millions of people of a particular nationality, subjugation of women, the rampant number of divorces that destroy family units, rapes and violence that treat women as inhuman, confusion of genders, racial discrimination, and pedophilia sins against children have been the result of fallen man and fallen woman's depravity.

Dominion over other human beings continue to this day in violation of God's creative dominion mandate of God. The immortal female functioning soul of both fallen man and woman became carnal and no longer spiritual. The immortal female functioning soul had no other choice but to allow the mortal male functioning body to gather stimuli from the physical world, so the immortal female functioning soul could be nourished with stimuli that fed the mind, emotions, and heart. The posterity of the first man and first woman were born without a vital participating immortal male functioning spirit, so the only one left that was providing stimuli to the female functioning soul was the mortal male functioning body.

Adam's act of disobedience was not the result of deception but was an intentional act of high treason because God told him directly not to eat the forbidden fruit. This is even clearer in Genesis 3:17 when God declared the causative reason Adam sinned was not because he had been deceived to sin: "Then to Adam He said, 'Because you have heeded the voice of your wife ....'" Although Adam did not heed the voice of the devil through the dragon, he had heeded the voice of his wife instead of the voice of God. Since Eve was the "weaker vessel" physically (1 Peter 3:7) and Adam did not correctly transmit to her what God said to him about not eating the forbidden fruit, Eve was deceived by the dragon. However, since Adam heeded the voice of his wife, the act resulted in Adam committing high treason.

Hence, it was not woman's weakness that caused her to sin, because God did not build into the woman or man the propensity or tendency to sin but created in the immortal female functioning soul merely a free will to choose to obey or not obey God's commands. God made the man and woman as moral agents with free wills who originally were not bent toward evil. It was Eve's desire to have self-exaltation to be like God in knowing good and evil, and Adam's failure to effectively communicate to or instruct his wife what God had forbidden that contributed to Eve's sin and desire to know good and evil independently of God. At least the woman could point to the fact that she was deceived, unlike the man who knowingly and intentionally disobeyed God, which constituted high treason.

On the other hand, the male adam intentionally allowed his desire for his wife, his counterpart, complementary, perfectly fitted female adam to override God's commandment. In looking at his wife, the husband was reminded that he, too, was a weak vessel physically as compared to other created animals living on earth. Yet, the male adam saw that the female adam was the only one on earth that was like him and came from his own body. Since the female adam ate the forbidden fruit and still was alive, the male adam became very curious and desirous of this new knowledge that the female adam had that he yet did not have. So, he too ate the forbidden fruit in rebellion against God.

Therefore, the male man felt that he should be sympathetic with the physically weaker, frailer, and more delicate vessel in the body, of the female adam. A male adam's roughness and virility in his body did not give him the strength to save himself, and most female adam's bodies statistically live longer than male adam's bodies, anyway. The male adam's toughness makes him more suited for public interaction in a hostile physical fallen environment full of, rough terrain, wild animals, creeping things on the ground, and the physical work assignments; but the influence of the female adam's artistic sensitivity makes the male adam to stop to smell the roses and contemplate and meditate on God's goodness, purpose, and beauty occasionally.

However, men and women are both functioning males in their immortal male functioning spirits and mortal male functioning bodies and immortal female functioning souls. In the natural, some of the most aggressive people in business are women. Some of these women cage fighters can easily knock out a man. Generally, unless led by the Holy Spirit, this aggression is expressing the male characteristics of the mortal male functioning body and are works of the flesh (Galatians 5:19-21) influencing the immortal female functioning soul.

To their credit, often women are the most aggressive in spiritual warfare against the kingdom of darkness. This Godly warfare aggression by the immortal female functioning soul in the spiritual realm is allowed under the authority of the immortal male functioning born again spirit in the woman and operates through the authority of Jesus and the power and the fruit of the Holy Spirit. Similarly, most great artists or musicians who see the beauty of God's creation include men because they have tapped into the sensitivity of their immortal female functioning souls.

Adam Was More Responsible For The Fall: Again, the man could not use as an excuse that he was deceived by the dragon like the woman. 1 Timothy 2:14 reveals a historical truth: "And Adam was not deceived, but the woman being deceived, fell into transgression." Eve was beguiled by the dragon's craftiness (2 Corinthians 11:3). Adam was more responsible because he committed sin without being deceived.

Having representative headship by virtue of being first created, and by the fact he was the only one receiving the prohibition directly from God, Adam was more responsible than Eve for bringing the wages of sin, which was death, to all mankind (Romans 5:12-21; Romans 6:23; 1 Corinthians 15-21-23). So, why is Eve in religious circles regularly charged with greater responsibility for the fall of humankind in the Garden of Eden?

Who then was the more culpable, the man or the woman? In church history 1 Timothy 2:14 has been used to subjugate church women, spiritually arguing that Eve was weaker than Adam since Eve was deceived and can still be deceived by evil spirits. Yet, these same historians fail to say that Adam was even weaker than Eve because he fell for the lustful desire for Eve or lust of the flesh with full knowledge of his wrongdoing. At least today the Believer wife seems to have special knowledge to watch out for the deceiving devil and the lustful flesh, although a Believer husband seems more prone to ignore the deadliness of the lustful flesh and the temptations in the world under the sway of the devil. "The wages of sin is death" (Romans 6:23).

In summary, the first man failed in his God-ordained stewardship responsibilities as a husband and marital head by virtue of being first created even before he ate the forbidden fruit because he failed to teach properly God's word to the first woman, his wife. Man was given woman as a complementary helper to make up for any of his deficiencies to better take dominion jointly over the entire earth and the living things on the earth; and the man and woman both were drawn to the physical world daily in their God-ordained work (Genesis 1:26-28). Their occupation, vocation, and mission were to steward God's physical earthly creation, but they became prideful about their job and lusted after the creation, ignoring the command of the Creator.

Since Eve succumbed to the dragon's temptation, and Adam chose his wife's affection over God's love and commandment, they equally sinned in their spirits, souls, and bodies. Since sin was committed by their entire beings, the sin produced total depravity and degeneration in all future mankind born.

The fallen immortal male functioning spirit and the fallen immortal female functioning soul of the male man and the female man were still immortal, and destined, unless redeemed, to punishment in the infernal Lake of Fire on the day of the White Throne Judgment (Revelation 20:15). Adam and Eve were functioning primarily with their natural psuche life of their immortal female functioning souls and the sarx or soma life of their mortal male functioning bodies, but then immortal male functioning spirits lost consciousness, were asleep, in a coma, were dead unto sins, and were no longer functioning.

Adam and Eve both had vibrant immortal female functioning souls, and mortal male functioning bodies, even after they sinned. They suffered death's intrusion that immediately started its degenerative work in each part of their triune being. They consequently equally took on the sinful nature and the desires of their new father, the devil in their immortal female functioning souls and mortal male functioning bodies. Since both Adam and Eve were treated equally by God in sentencing them to infernal death as the consequences of their disobedience, the possibility of salvation unto everlasting life in Christ Jesus also was given to them equally. Until the appearance of the Messiah, man and woman both equally, along with the whole world were under the sway of the devil after the fall (1 John 5:18-19). Verses 18 & 19 says; (18) We know that whosoever is born of God sinneth not; but he that is begotten of God keepeth himself, and that wicked one toucheth him not. (19) And we know that we are of God, and the whole world lieth in wickedness."

Jesus spoke to the religious leaders and in John 8:44 He chastised: "Ye are of your father the devil, and the lusts of your father ye will do. He was a murderer from the beginning, and abode not in the truth, because there is no truth in him. When he speaketh a lie, he speaketh of his own: for he is a liar, and the father of it."

Murder is a crime under the law to kill the mortal male functioning body, which houses the immortal male functioning born again spirit and the immortal female functioning soul, but calling somebody a "good for nothing" or "fool" has equal punishment under God's kingdom principles since it attacks the immortal male functioning born again spirit and the immortal female functioning soul (Matthew 5:22).

Similarly, a lie is an assault against someone's character, and in the kingdom of God this causes the process of death to start working in the immortal female functioning soul because only truth should be allowed.

Adultery with the mortal male functioning body was a crime under the law, but lust in the heart in the immortal female functioning soul was an equal sin in the Kingdom of God, as the mortal male functioning body can do nothing unless he is told to do it by the soul exercising the will (Matthew 5:20-30).

The original father of sins acted out by the mortal male functioning body and the immortal female functioning soul was the devil (John 8:44). Romans 5:12, 14 says, "Therefore, just as through one man sin entered the world, and death through sin, and thus death spread to all men, because all sinned- ...Nevertheless death reigned from Adam to Moses...." God said death entered the world through one man. Adam and Eve in their oneness sinned against God, but the male Adam was the more culpable.

Fallen man and woman's once vibrant and strong immortal male functioning spirits indivisibly were welded into their immortal female functioning souls. This is why in Hebrews 4:12 the Word (the logos becoming alive and changing to the rhema) of God is said to be sharper than a two-edged sword able to divide asunder soul from spirit. Fallen mankind became naturally sinful, became totally devoid and destitute of righteousness, and became sons of the devil instead of sons of God. Mankind changed families in the spirit realm by the disobedient act of their wills, which were choices ultimately made by the immortal female functioning souls of mankind where the will and heart live and function. Before the fall the immortal female functioning soul had total agreement with the immortal male functioning spirit and mortal male functioning body regarding their dominion duties and mission granted to them by God.

The fallen immortal female functioning soul had earthly knowledge and wisdom, receiving knowledge through the five senses of the mortal male functioning body unless the still voice come from God or temptation from an evil spirit. Except for prophets, the immortal female functioning soul became carnal and no longer had perfect communion with God, and no longer was being led by the sinless immortal male functioning spirit. Fallen man and woman were now self-conscious and sensory-conscious but no longer spiritually conscious as part of their daily living.

Unrestrained by their immortal male functioning spirits and no longer having the daily visits with God, after the fall, the man and woman's female functioning souls forgot the purity which they were originally created in the image and likeness of God as a complementary helper to man and woman's immortal male functioning spirits (Genesis 1:26,27). Their immortal female functioning souls were now subject to temptations from within by their fallen sin nature, from without by the mortal male functioning body living in the fallen world, and by the demonic forces in the kingdom of darkness unless their immortal female functioning souls responded to the evident goodness of God (Romans 2:4). Their immortal female functioning souls now had Satan's twisted fallen knowledge and wisdom of good and evil operating in them. Their mortal male functioning bodies now had the sin principle, itself, dwelling in their members of their bodies (Romans 7:18).

Losing their intimate communion with God, fallen man and woman's true essence, their immortal male functioning spirit, which was the "lamp of the Lord" (Proverbs 20:27) was lost into darkness.

In the immortal female functioning soul, fallen mankind's mind (thought center), emotions (feelings center), and heart (belief center) became self-centered instead of God-centered. The immortal female functioning soul was not regularly receiving divine spiritual truth or inspirational words from God; so, the immortal female functioning soul's mind producing thoughts became carnal, the emotions producing feelings became unstable, and the heart producing false beliefs in idols, unbelief in God, and believed that she was a god. So, the immortal female functioning soul's mind, emotions, and heart started accepting as reality and fact the carnal knowledge transmitted by the mortal male functioning body's five senses of the stimuli from the physical world as the reality of life, along with demonic voices and temptations, instead of believing and seeking spiritual communication with God.

The mortal male functioning body was subject to perverted animal-like instincts, cravings, diseases, frailties, sicknesses, infirmities, and death, which were the wages being paid for the sins he committed with the immortal female functioning souls (Romans 6:23).

The fallen immortal female functioning soul became mentally and emotionally ill, with demonic wisdom, fleshly, lustful thoughts, unstable emotions, false idols and beliefs, and a will to habitually sin against God.

Romans 11:29 says, "For the gifts and calling of God are without repentance." When the first man and woman fell into sin and lost their daily communion with God, they experienced not only the process of dying, but still had their stewardship dominion responsibilities over the earth and care for all created things living in the gravitational pull of the earth (Genesis 3:22-23), but they had to do it without the continuous communication and fellowship with God; and they both were under the authority of the prince of this world (John 14:30; Ephesians 2:2).

The devil usurped Adam and Eve's dominion possessory authority over the earth, and the things on the earth; and the man and woman came under the authority of the devil who was now the prince of the world. The realm of man and woman's delegated authority originally granted by God came under the devil's curse as their relationship with the all-powerful God was separated and diminished. When man and woman's intimate communion with God terminated, and the immortal male functioning spirit died in sins or became unconscious not exhibiting spiritual life, man and woman lost God's spiritual communion and intimate relationship.

However, the devil became their new evil and deceptive father (John 8:44), but the devil had to rule over people through mankind because the devil did not have a body to do physical things as did mankind because it took viable spirits or souls inside bodies formed from the dust of the ground by God to exercise dominion authority over the earth (Genesis 1:26-28; 2:7; 2:21-23,; 3:17-22). The devil was merely a fallen, rebellious spirit already under judgment, but was waiting for the White Throne judgment day when God threw him in the Lake of Fire (Revelation 20:10).

The Last Adam and Second Man: The disobedient deeds of the most culpable man, Adam, and the righteous deeds of our Lord and Savior, Jesus Christ, affected many people. Adam's disobedience resulted in condemnation and death, whereas Jesus' obedience, as the Last Adam and Second Man resulted in justification and eternal life (Romans 5:12-21). Adam is the natural head and father of the old creation race, while Jesus is the spiritual Head and Father of the new creation race. Since all natural descendants of Adam, whether male or female, are born with a sin nature, then Jesus in John 3:3-8 discussed with Nicodemus how he must be born again to receive a new spirit that is alive and vibrant to see and enter the Kingdom of God.

Jesus' humanity nature was different than any other human in that He was not born with a sin nature, nor did He ever yield to temptation and sin; so, the Apostle Paul referred to Jesus as the "Last Adam" and the "Second Man" (1 Corinthians 15:45-47). Jesus is the spiritual DNA everlasting Father of the born again New Man (Isaiah 9:6; 1 Peter 1:23), not a refurbishment of the Old Man from Adam but a whole born again New Creation in Christ Jesus (2 Corinthians 5:17) that did not sin (1 John 3:9), and was absolutely righteous and holy (Ephesians 4:24).

Sin was a deadly intrusion into the male adam and female adam's innocent, immortal male functioning spirits and immortal female functioning souls and mortal male functioning bodies. "For the wages of sin is death..." (Romans 6:23). Sin is not essential to human nature, and contrary to the teaching of Gnostics, flesh, without the intrusion of sin, was not originally created as inherently evil. Thus, Jesus, as the Seed (Galatians 3:19; 1 Peter 1:23) in existence before the foundation of the world (John 8:58; 17:5,24; Colossians 1:17; Revelation 22:13), was begotten of God as sinless in His humanity nature, and while Jesus lived here on earth, was tempted in all things and yet did not sin (Hebrews 4:15).

The Woman did not become a 2nd class citizen after the fall of Mankind

Chapter Three

CHAPTER THREE

The Woman Did Not Become a Second Class Citizen After the Fall of Mankind

Let us return to Genesis 3 and see what happened after first the woman and then the man ate the forbidden fruit. What was the first act that the man and woman did after they sinned?

Genesis 3:7 says, "And the eyes of them both were opened, and they knew that they were naked; and they sewed fig leaves together and made themselves aprons." Naked means you are not clothed. Why was nakedness such a problem? They had always been naked since creation. There were no other people around that would cause them to be ashamed. God created them, so that should not cause them to be ashamed.

Before the fall, Adam and Eve were clothed with the presence of God's created glory light for mankind, and their soulish eyes perceived the spiritual glory God put in His created things and order. In fact, before the fall, man and woman's soulish eyes perceived their physical bodies clothed in God's glory light, and their spirits saw into the spiritual realm the beauty of God's creation.

God anointed glory on everything He created: 1 Corinthians 15: 40-41 says, "There are also celestial bodies (stars, suns, moons), and bodies terrestrial (every created thing on earth): but the glory of the celestial is one, and the glory of the terrestrial is another. (41) There is one glory of the sun, and another glory of the moon, and another glory of the stars: for one star different from another star in glory."

After the fall, Adam and Eve's eyes of their immortal female functioning souls were opened to perceived information only from the physical world unclothed without their created glory light of God that had protected their innocence and allowed them to see into the spiritual world. They saw that they were no longer clothed. They lost the ability to see the glory light on God's creation.

Genesis 3:8-10 says, "And they heard the voice of the LORD God walking in the garden in the cool of the day: and Adam and his wife hid themselves from the presence of the LORD God amongst the trees of the garden. (9) And the LORD God called unto Adam, and said unto Him, 'Where art thou?' (10) And he (Adam) said, 'I heard Thy voice in the garden, and I was afraid, because I was naked; and I hid myself.'"

God had to stop speaking as the Father and had to start speaking as the Judge because three beings in God's garden broke the law of His Kingdom. God's sense of justice and the integrity of His word spoken in Genesis 2:17 was violated. God's commandment was, "But of the tree of the knowledge of good and evil, thou shalt not eat of it: for in the day that thou eatest thereof thou shalt surely die."

By the fall in Genesis 3, God's requirement for man and woman to maintain sinlessness, righteousness, and holiness were violated, so God's sense of justice had to be satisfied. Adam and Eve could choose to break God's commandment, but they had no authority to choose the consequences of breaking God's commandment.

God hates sin, and His justice mandates that He deal with created beings who commit sin. Adam and Eve not only committed sin by eating the forbidden fruit to make themselves independent of God, but they also committed sin by disobeying God not to eat the forbidden fruit regardless of their motive. God is holy, just, and forgiving; but God is also all knowing, and He already had a plan to bring forgiveness and reconciliation with fallen man. Adam and Eve's sin did not catch God by surprise. Since God is all knowing, He knew that Eve would be deceived by the dragon, and He knew that Adam would choose keeping the affection of his wife of more importance than obeying God. God is not restricted by time, so He went forward and saw Lucifer's fall, Satan's use of the dragon to deceive Eve to commit sin and Adam's sin of affection of his wife. Yet, God had begotten His Son Jesus before the foundation of the world that would return God's Kingdom to earth, defeat the devil, bring salvation to mankind, and start a new creation of human beings.

God's sense of divine justice that God cannot violate required Him to bring death in the lives of the fallen Adam and fallen Eve. God's justice required Adam to suffer with hard labor in his work to care for his family, and God's justice required Eve to suffer during the birth of children.

Genesis 3:11, "And God said, 'Who told thee that thou wast naked? Hast thou eaten of the tree, whereof I commanded thee that thou shouldest not eat?", of course, God already knew the truth.

Then, the man knew he had sinned for not rebuking the dragon and failure of ordering his wife not to eat the forbidden fruit; but instead, as a defense the man started the blame game for committing sin, Genesis 3:12, "And the man said, 'The woman whom thou gavest to be with me, she gave me of the tree, and I did eat." So, Adam blamed God and the woman for his high treason sin.

Then God turned to the woman in Genesis 3:13, "And the LORD God said unto the woman, 'What is this that thou hast done?' And the woman said, 'The serpent beguiled me, and I did eat.'"

So, the woman did not blame her husband for failing to teach her correctly of God's commandment not to eat the forbidden fruit or for failing to protect her while the dragon was deceiving her. Often, the wife protects her husband even when he is wrong. The wife here just blamed the devil and not her husband, Adam. How many times have we seen or heard of a wife even being assaulted by her husband not saying anything bad about the husband to the police, or later telling the criminal prosecutor that she does not want to prosecute her husband for his wrong committed.

Genesis 3:14 says, "And the LORD God said unto the serpent (dragon), 'Because thou hast done this, thou art cursed above all cattle, and above every beast of the field; upon thy belly shalt thou go, and dust shalt thou eat all the days of thy life." God knew that the devil was speaking through the dragon, and He said that the dragon would eat the dust of the ground. Serpents eat mice and small animals, not dust. Dragons eat pigs, Timor deer, buffalo, snakes, and fish that wash up on the shore but not the dust of the ground.

Here is a curious perspective. What was made by dust from the ground? It was animals, birds, fish, and human beings. What God was saying was that the devil and demons would be at enmity with mankind. Later in Genesis 6 we read how the fallen angels came down and entered the daughters of Adam and Eve and begat men of reknown (gibbor). There were also giants on the earth at that time. When the giants and men of renown died, their spirits became the demons as disembodied spirits were able to enter physical bodies of animals and humans. Jesus cast out demons inside people regularly throughout His ministry. After casting out legions of demons out of a man, Jesus gave permission to the demons to enter about 2000 pigs, where the pigs were driven down a steep hill where they drown in the sea (Mark 5:11-13).

In Genesis 3:15 God spoke further judgment against the devil, "And I will put enmity between thee and the woman, and between thy seed and her Seed; He shall bruise thy head, and thou shalt bruise His heel."

Without question, this was God's promise of a coming Redeemer where a virgin woman's Seed would crush the "headship" of the devil. 1 John 3:8 says, "He that committeth sin is of the devil; for the devil sinneth from the beginning. For this purpose the Son of God was manifested, that he might destroy the works of the devil."

Since a woman does not produce a seed, but rather an egg, then this also was a reference of a virgin birth and that the Seed would be implanted by God (Luke 1:26-35). Isaiah 7:14 says, "Therefore the Lord himself shall give you a sign; 'Behold, a virgin shall conceive, and bear a Son, and shall call His name Immanuel.'"

Genesis 3:16, "Unto the woman He said, 'I will greatly multiply thy sorrow and thy conception; in sorrow thou shalt bring forth children; and thy desire shall be to thy husband, and he shall rule (wife has to submit in a godly manner) over thee."

Although she did suffer the consequences of her sin through pain in childbirth, the woman's posterity was honored to be chosen to give birth to the Messiah, the holy sinless Seed of God that was implanted in the womb of the Virgin, Mary. Bringing forth children would be painful for the woman, but she desires children, and the mother's heart is full of joy and the pain of birth is secondary.

Being submissive to her husband, the wife can teach her husband how to be submissive as the Betrothed of Christ by her own submission to her husband, which some men naturally find it difficult to submit to God for a season. A righteous man lays down his life for his spouse as Christ did for His Church. Ephesians 5:23, 25 says, "For the husband is the head of the wife, even as (no more and no less than) Christ is the head of the church: and He is the Saviour of the body… (25) Husbands, love your wives, even as Christ also loved the church, and gave himself for it." 1 Peter 3:7 says, "Likewise, ye husbands, dwell with your wife according to knowledge, giving honor unto the wife, as unto the weaker vessel, and as being heirs together of the grace of life; that your prayers be not hindered."

Genesis 3:17, "And unto Adam he said, 'Because thou hast hearkened unto the voice of thy wife, and hast eaten of the tree, of which I commanded thee, saying, 'Thou shalt not eat of it: cursed is the ground (but not curse of Adam) for thy sake; in sorrow shalt thou eat of it all the days of thy life; (18) Thorns also and thistles shall it bring forth to thee; and thou shalt eat the herb of the field; (19) In the sweat of thy face shalt thou eat bread, till thou return unto the ground; for out of it was thou taken: for dust thou art, and unto dust shalt thou return."

This was when the ground and nature were cursed, but the man was not cursed. Although the husband did not heed the voice of devil behind the dragon or God, he did heed the voice of his wife instead; and he thereby committed high treason in God's spiritual Kingdom.

Men suffer from working their entire lives. Without question, women in the workplace also suffer from the pressures of a job or profession. Yet, in an agrarian culture at the time of Adam and Eve, and their upcoming posterity, men normally had the primary job of tilling the ground, planting, cultivating, and harvesting crops, along with caring and shearing sheep, and caring and milking goats, cows, etc.

Genesis 3:20 says, "And Adam called his wife's name, Eve because she was the mother of all living." So, Adam named his wife, Eve because based on what God said in Genesis 3:15, she was not the mother of the dying, but rather was the mother of the living. Great honor was bestowed upon Eve, as she became the mother of all children that would be born thereafter on earth, especially the birth of the Messiah, Jesus Christ, fulfilling God's mandate in Genesis 1:28 to be fruitful and multiply. Thus, God confirmed that Adam and Eve would continue to work for God in creating new spiritual beings which the devil could not do.

It seems strange at first why Adam named his wife Eve, the mother of all living when they just committed a sin that brought death to themselves and all their future posterity. Adam had faith. Why? Faith comes by hearing and hearing by the rhema of God (Romans 10:17). Because Adam just heard God say that through his wife's descendant daughters that one of them will be a virgin who gives birth to a child and God's Son (Isaiah 9:6), who would be born as the King, the Redeemer, the Savior, the Messiah who would destroy the headship authority of the king of the kingdom of darkness, the devil, and would get back the possession of the world for God the Father (1 John 3:8).

Psalms 2:8 says, "Ask of me, and I shall give Thee (Christ Jesus) the heathen for Thine inheritance, and the uttermost parts of the earth for Thy possession." This verse prophesies that God was going to give, and did give, the earth to His only begotten Son, Christ Jesus, as His possession and the nations of peoples as His inheritance. Therefore, the earth along with every nation on the earth are under the rulership of the Son King, Jesus. Revelations 11:15 says, "And the seventh angel sounded; and there were great voices in heaven, saying, 'The kingdoms of this world are become the kingdoms of our Lord, and of His Christ; and He (Christ) shall reign for ever and ever.'"

Thus, Adam saw future hope for everlasting life, not death in God's chastisement and that that Adam and Eve's posterity, through God's Christ, the Messiah, would be saved and will be part of the family of God; and with Son of God and child of the virgin, shall possess the entire earth and rule every nation of people on the earth. Thus, Adam and Eve had great hope for the future. Revelation 5:10 says, "And hast made us unto our God kings and priests: and we shall reign on the earth." Adam and Eve's future posterity who become Believers of this Redeemer and God's Son, born of Adam and Eve's future virgin woman great, great great, etc. granddaughter, and will allow Adam and Eve's posterity to rule and reign here on earth with this Son of God and man's Redeemer forever.

Isaiah's prophecy of the coming Messiah in 9: 6-7, says, "For unto us a child is born, unto us a Son is given: and the government shall be upon His shoulder: and His name shall be called Wonderful, Counsellor, The mighty God, The everlasting Father, The Prince of Peace. (7) Of the increase of His government and peace there shall be no end, upon the throne of David, and upon His kingdom, to order it, and to establish it with judgment and with justice from henceforth even forever. The zeal of the LORD of hosts will perform this."

Since the holy Seed that impregnated the virgin in Genesis 3:15 would not come from a man, it must come from God; thus, this Seed will be from God and will fertilize the egg of the virgin woman. He will be known as the Son of God, the Son of man, and the child of the blessed virgin woman. The birth of this Son of God Who was sent to earth to save fallen mankind and Who would crush the headship authority of the devil was given to a virgin woman, a descendant of Adam and Eve. This was the greatest honor given to a human, and it was given to a virtuous woman, not a man.

For God to stay true to His sense of justice, then the Son of God and man's Redeemer had to have been begotten of God before both the devil, mankind, and the entire spiritual and natural worlds were created. Jesus said in John 17:5, "And now, O Father, glorify Thou Me with Thine own self with the glory which I had with Thee before the world was." To be the Son of God and the child of the virgin woman, this Son of God and man's Redeemer had to have both a divine nature and a humanity nature, where His birth here on earth had to be planned; and those men and women who would be redeemed and saved had to be known by God before the foundation and creation of both the natural and spiritual worlds (Ephesians 1:4-5; John 17:5; Revelations 13:8). Thus, Adam and Eve rejoiced that their descendants who accept God's miracle birth Son will have everlasting life and not infernal death (John 3:16). So, Adam in Genesis 3:20 named his wife, Eve, the mother of the living, not the mother of the dead.

Genesis 3:21 says, "Unto Adam also and to his wife did the LORD God make coats of skins and clothed them."

Genesis 3:21 dealt with the requirement from that time onward that a death and spilling of blood was required as a sacrifice of the innocent for the atonement for sins committed by Adam and Eve and their posterity thereafter. Until sin entered the world no sacrifices were required to be offered for the man and woman. God taught Adam and Eve that without shedding of innocent blood there would be no temporary remission of sin, but that God will accept the vicarious sacrifice of innocent animals until the Messiah whose heel would be bruised by the dragon would come in the future as mentioned in Genesis 3:15 to offer Himself to die a vicarious death as God's chosen Sacrificial Lamb for the eternal remission of sins of mankind. Until Messiah comes, the temporary sacrifice of innocent animals shows also that the innocence of Adam and Eve was gone.

Before the fall, Adam had named the animals and tamed them and some he made them pets; but now Adam must have felt guilty that an innocent animal would have to be slain as an atonement to cover his sins and his wife's sins. Adam surely thought that the Redeemer mentioned by God in Genesis 3:15 would have to be slain for mankind's eternal remission of sin because atonement required, according to God, the spilling of innocent blood. Thus, the sacrifice of innocent animals was simply a temporary atonement of sins which practice would have to continue to satisfy God's justice until God's Son and the virgin woman's child is crucified on the Roman Cross.

Genesis 3:22-24 says, "Then the Lord God said, `Behold, the man has become like one of Us, to know good and evil (in man's soul). And now, lest he put out his hand (man's body) and take also of the tree of life, and eat, and live forever'-- therefore the Lord God sent him (the mortal male functioning body of Adam and Eve) out of the Garden of Eden to till the ground from which he was taken. So, He drove out the man (generic man and woman); and He placed cherubim at the east of the garden of Eden, and a flaming sword which turned every way, to guard the way to the Tree of Life."

Did the male man have to leave the Garden of Eden, but the female man be allowed to stay? No! The man and woman were both driven out of the Garden of Eden; so, why did God just mention the man? It is suggested that the reason was that both Adam and Eve had mortal male functioning bodies. God referred only to the mortal male functioning body because the immortal female functioning soul was already immortal, and she already was destined to die an infernal everlasting death unless saved by God's Son as prophesied in Genesis 3:15.

Yet, the mortal male functioning body of both Adam and Eve would decay back to the ground unless their mortal male functioning bodies ate from the Tree of Life. However, it was God's mercy that forbade it. At that time, Adam and Eve's mortal male functioning bodies wrongfully would have obtained immortality with an unredeemable sin nature if the mortal male functioning body had eaten from the Tree of Life. Thus, God exercised mercy and drove the mortal male functioning bodies of both Adam and Eve out of the Garden to protect their mortal male functioning bodies from unredeemable infernal damnation. Fortunately, Believers will receive a new resurrected body that is a new creation like Jesus' resurrected new creation body when Jesus returns back to earth (1 Corinthians 15:23). This new creation body will be immortal, incorruptible, glorious, powerful, and spiritual, to live perfectly in and when the new heaven and new earth are joined together (1 Corinthians 15:42-44; Revelation chapter 21).

Also, God saw the potential in the mortal male functioning body as God's Temple (1 Corinthians 3:16; 2 Corinthians 6;16; Ephesians 2;21) in the future after redemption and saw His only begotten Son paying the price for an immortal spiritual male function body upon the Son's return to earth after His death, resurrection, and ascension (1 Corinthians 15:23, 52-56).

Summary of the Relationship between Man's triune nature: What was the relationship before the fall between the immortal male functioning spirit, the immortal female functioning soul, and the mortal male functioning mortal body? Before the fall the mortal male functioning body of both Adam and Eve merely functioned as the butler protecting, and subduing the natural world per the dictates of the immortal male functioning spirit and the immortal female functioning soul.

The immortal male functioning spirit was the husband of his wife, the immortal female functioning soul, where the mind, emotions, and will in the heart reside. Again, before the fall, the immortal female functioning soul received either spiritual knowledge and experiences as stimuli from the immortal male functioning spirit who had access to God's spiritual world or received natural knowledge and experiences as stimuli from the five senses of the mortal male functioning body who lived in the natural world.

The fall of mankind caused death, divorce, and strained relations between man and woman. Since all knowledge is received through relationship, the mortal male functioning body and immortal female functioning soul had to live with each other; and the mortal male functioning body became the immortal female functioning soul's new provider of knowledge, emotions, and beliefs stimuli from the natural world. The immortal female functioning soul no longer was receiving spiritual knowledge, wisdom, and truths from God's spiritual kingdom because the immortal male functioning spirit was asleep in a coma.

The immortal female functioning soul's dependence upon the mortal male functioning body for nourishment forced them to set up house having an unspiritual and deceptively carnal relationship. The relationship between the immortal female functioning soul and the mortal male functioning body caused frustration, stress, and unrealistic demands placed upon each other, leaving dissatisfaction and unfulfilled existence for both the immortal female functioning soul and the mortal male functioning body.

Because the mortal male functioning body learned that the immortal female functioning soul was dependent upon the mortal male functioning body for knowledge, emotions, and belief stimulation, the mortal male functioning body became domineering over the immortal female functioning soul. The mortal male functioning body only offered the immortal female functioning soul the lusts of the flesh or lust of the eyes as food for intellectual, emotional, and beliefs that satisfied the mortal male functioning body's desires but could never satisfy the immortal female functioning soul's pride of life and aspirations for a higher life to live than the physical world offers.

In the fallen state, only the immortal female functioning soul is the one who can accept Jesus as Lord and Savior. At best, Adam and Eve were told by God, Himself, that a Redeemer, God's only begotten Son and the child of the virgin woman was qualified to be King of God's Kingdom and Redeemer of fallen mankind through man and woman's repentance and the remission of sins, who would be King of God's Kingdom, and who would defeat the devil and the kingdom of darkness.

God told the female man in Genesis 3:16 that "'I will greatly multiply thy sorrow and thy conception; in sorrow thou shalt bring forth children; and thy desire shall be to thy husband, and he shall rule (wife must submit) over thee."

The word sorrow is of the immortal female functioning soul, whereas pain is a response from the central nervous system of the body. After the fall, the immortal male functioning spirit in both man and woman was welded into their immortal female functioning souls, having immediately experienced death unto sins or unconsciousness upon man committing sin. The persons that were still functionally alive in man's triune nature were the beastly mortal male functioning body and the immortal female functioning soul who was a princess. Therefore, God's prophecy, or word of judgment, was directed to the immortal female functioning soul and the mortal male functioning body, not the dead or unconscious immortal male functioning spirit. God's pronouncement was to those parts of Adam and Eve which were still alive and functioning as female and male in their triune creative designs.

In Genesis 3:16, the word desire in the Hebrew is tesshuwqah which is the same word used in Genesis 4:7 when God spoke to Cain before he murdered Abel. God said, "If you do well, will you not be accepted? And if you do not do well, sin lies at the door. And its desire (tesshuwqah) is for you, but you should rule over it." Because mankind suddenly knew fallen good and evil, the man and woman had the capacity to do evil or to do things that seem good to self. Yet, God told Cain that sin was like a large beastly cat that was crouching down ready to pounce on Cain. This is the type of unwholesome desire that Eve would have for her husband because she wanted to fulfill God's mandate to be fruitful and mulitply. She wanted to use her natural looks and actions to attract her husband.

Mankind became disobedient and self-centered instead of being obedient and God-centered. This was the first reference after the fall that God had a body of law governing man's activities. Yet, one cannot conclude that the immortal female functioning soul's fallen desire and the mortal male functioning body's fallen rule were to punish the immortal female functioning soul or woman and reward the male flesh.

Woman was not punished for her deeds, while the man was rewarded for his disobedience, especially since the man's actions were the more culpable. God merely was saying there will be conflict between the immortal female functioning soul whose desire would be to receive knowledge, emotions, and beliefs stimuli from her new husband, the mortal male functioning body. Although God was speaking to Eve and Adam, He was speaking to all women and men born as their posterity but also was speaking about the mortal male functioning bodies and female functioning souls of both Eve and Adam.

On the other hand, the mortal male functioning body would try to rule over the immortal female functioning soul in contradiction to the created order of an immortal being better than a mortal. Because the immortal female functioning soul was trapped inside she could not encounter the physical environment directly, so she had to often submit to the mortal male functioning body. The fallen immortal female functioning soul had to relegate herself to being just a receiver of knowledge, emotions, and beliefs stimuli only from the physical world and had to exercise the will based upon the stimuli that was given to the princess by the fallen mortal male functioning body. Thus, the immortal female functioning soul became carnally minded, emotionally unstable, and willfully disobedient in her heart towards God. The mortal male functioning body's carnal stimuli from the fallen world was all the immortal female functioning soul had for food, unless the immortal female functioning soul looked for another provider of stimuli.

There are demons that tempt the immortal female functioning soul with evil stimuli and false religions from the kingdom of darkness ruled by Satan. These demonic powers would work in the world environment under the sway and control of the devil, as the prince of this world, continuously keeping the mortal male functioning body in the bondage of sin. Eventually, the sin principle, itself, started residing in the mortal male functioning body, and upon salvation through Christ Jesus the mortal male functioning body with its flesh has to be pruned out of the immortal female functioning soul by Father God to bear more fruit (John 15:2), washed and sanctified to remove the dirt of the flesh out of the immortal female functioning soul by God the Word (Ephesians 5:26), and mortified the deeds of the flesh in the immortal female functioning of the soul by the Holy Spirit to gain more zoe life (Romans 8:13). The immortal female functioning soul must be rid of the mortal male functioning body's passions and desires (Romans 6:6; Galatians 2:20; 5:24).

But now the immortal female functioning soul and the mortal male functioning body had to live in a world that was under the rulership of the usurping prince of this world who stole their possessory, stewardship rights of the earth and all things living on the earth (John 14:30). To a similar manner, the mortal male functioning body as the butler for the royal immortals was created only to be a servant to the immortal male functioning spirit and the immortal female functioning soul to help them exercise stewardship rule over God's creation.

Since the immortal male functioning spirit was "dead unto sins" or unconscious, the immortal female functioning soul's new provider of stimuli was lust fulfilling, beer drinking, burping, habit developing unspiritual mortal male functioning body.

The immortal female functioning soul's desire was to continue in the rulership status she had over the mortal male functioning body when the immortal male functioning spirit was still alive and not dead in sins or unconscious. However, God's sentence to the immortal female functioning soul was that her new provider would rule over her since she must have knowledge and emotional stimulation as food to live just as the mortal male functioning body needed bread, fruits, vegetables, and meat and water as food to live. Unfortunately, the mortal male functioning body could only offer to the immortal female functioning soul stimuli of a carnal lifestyle, with the mortal male functioning body's hereditary mortal limitations.

This new order of rulership was backwards and was not God's best. This was a mortal male functioning body ruling over an immortal female functioning soul. The relationship was like the "Planet of the Apes" ruling over humans. The authority was upside down. It was a relationship like the "Beauty and the Beast." The marital headship and responsibility under God's prefect relationship by a sinless immortal male functioning spirit perfectly submitted to God, not a carnal lust-driven mortal male functioning body, limited by his mortality and attached only to the natural things of the world.

Whenever the man sinned in his flesh, the immortal female functioning soul found the experience and knowledge good temporarily to satisfy her self-centered hunger. Since the immortal female functioning soul had fallen by the devil's deception, she used her new knowledge of how to deceive to get the mortal male functioning body physically to do what was good for her self-fulfillment, self-image, and self-aggrandizement. However, what was the fallen good for the immortal female functioning soul's self-centeredness was evil sin under the Law of God. Making the moral male functioning body do those things that temporarily feel good, such as drugs, alcohol, illicit sex, false religions do lead to sickness and eventual death of the mortal male functioning body. This sinful activity confirms Newton's law of entropy, which is that everything in the physical world is tending toward decaying or dying or as Paul called it, the law of sin and death (Romans 8:2).

The immortal female functioning soul could never be satisfied with the physical knowledge and emotions about things in the world, as she was built from the immortal male functioning spirit by the breath of God (Genesis 2:7). This left a void or vacuum in the immortal female functioning soul, and she hungered after a spiritual experience of higher images, thoughts, and emotional highs to stimulate her. The immortal female functioning soul had a taste for the spiritual world to satisfy her hunger and thirst for things everlasting or that were immortal. Moreover, the immortal female functioning soul did not realize that this urge to obtain immortal or spiritual knowledge was put into her as a void by God, which can only be filled and satisfied by the all-knowing, all present, all-powerful God. In fact, this void could only be filled completely when the Godhead created in man an immortal male functioning born again spirit and took up residence in man (John 14:16; 23; 1 Peter 1:23).

Since the immortal female functioning soul had no way to obtain knowledge, feelings, and beliefs from the spiritual world because she was residing inside, spiritual things had to be brought to her. Therefore, the evil spirits of darkness saw the hunger and thirst of the immortal female functioning soul as an opportunity for entrance for influence, oppression, possession, and control. The untransformed immortal female functioning soul thirsted in her heart for spiritual companionship. Since the immortal female functioning soul was in sin, and the Redeemer yet had not appeared, the immortal female functioning soul could only satisfy her desire for spiritual companionship with the only spirits she encountered, which were the rebellious, deceitful, perverted evil spirits of the kingdom of darkness who enticed her with false religions.

Yet, when the immortal female functioning soul seeks transcendent knowledge and morality, God shows her His goodness, mercy, and grace through the death and resurrection of Jesus Christ. So, it is the transcendent goodness of God that leads the immortal female functioning soul to repentance (Romans 2:4).

Unfortunately, like a soap opera director, the devil played the mortal male functioning body's needs to fulfill the lusts of the flesh and lusts of the eyes against the immortal female functioning soul's needs to dominate her environment to satisfy her hunger for knowledge, emotional experience, and new beliefs as an immortal being. Thus, the immortal female functioning soul was and is in frequent conflict with the mortal male functioning body, which conflict continues even after the initial salvation experience (Romans 7:14-25). Fortunately, even from the beginning, God formed the creation, every living thing, and even the stars to testify of the Redeemer; so, the immortal female functioning soul could see the Messiah and accept His coming and suffering and dying for mankind. Thus, salvation was made available for the faithful of the Old Testament who looked forward to the coming Messiah and Redeemer and that the whole natural creation witnesses their is a God and Redeemer.

God created the immortal female functioning soul to hunger and thirst for a river of spiritual truth that could only be supplied by the One who is omniscient, God the Word, personified in Christ Jesus. God's purpose was never for men and women to fill their internal void or vacuum with temporal knowledge, since temporal knowledge is decaying or at best is temporary. Temporal physical knowledge keeps disappearing inside the void or vacuum as it is subject to the law of sin and death.

Only God's everlasting, eternal, and invisible spiritual knowledge and emotional fellowship through knowing God in Christ can fill the emptiness and not decay and die. The living Temple God chose to be His resting place was the mortal male functioning body made by God, Himself, from the dust of the ground.

God wanted to afford the descendants of Adam and Eve to have immortal male functioning born again spirits, and upon the Believer's death and resurrection, the Believer will receive an immortal spiritual body. God still wants to continue with His original creative plan that an immortal male functioning spirit, with an immortal female functioning soul, in a mortal functioning body would take dominion over the things of the earth under the stewardship authority of God, and eventually receiving an immortal male functioning body through Christ Jesus, God's plan is fulfilled.

Before salvation the immortal female functioning soul gave the mortal male functioning body permission to sin, choose for the mortal male functioning body what to eat and drink, when to sleep, decide what clothes to wear, what car to drive, what university to attend, what work career to endeavor, how to establish a budget, who to marry, how many children to have, what books to read, where to vacation, what to search on the internet, the names given to children, where to live, how to live, what to say during an argument, and when to physically defend yourself.

After salvation, the immortal female functioning soul does the above things but also orders the body to stop sinning, to travel to church, to raise holy hands in worship, attend home fellowship of the saints, pray, exercise spiritual gits, daily read and study the Bible, get rid of sinful relationships, develop close friendships with mature and dedicated Believers, and to humbly submit to the Godhead unto the transformation of the mind, emotions, and heart. Submit and seek daily to become the chaste Betrothed of the Lord, and be the holy temple of God. The mortal male functioning body must be presented as a living sacrifice, holy, acceptable unto God (Romans 12:1).

Eventually, it was the immortal female functioning soul who cried out to respond to God the Father pursuing for a renewal of her immortal female functioning soul; and the Father revealed to her His only begotten Son, Who was sent to be the Redeemer of all mankind; and that by receiving His only begotten Son as Lord and Savior that could fulfill the immortal female souls every search for spiritual fulfillment and a new spiritual companion (husband) or new born again spirit (John 3:3-5; 2 Corinthains 5:17).

Upon salvation, Christ's humanity nature gave to the immortal female functioning soul a new, sinless, perfect immortal male functioning born again spirit (1 Peter 1:23; Hebrews 12:23 1 John 3:9). God's plan of redemption included Jesus' mother, the Virgin Mary, who had an immortal female functioning soul, along with her mortal male functioning body to be the receptor for God's holy Seed, God's only begotten Son, planted in the virgin woman's womb to give birth to the Word became flesh and dwelt amongst us (John 1:14). Jesus had a sinless immortal male functioning spirit, a sinless immortal female functioning soul, and a sinless mortal male functioning body. Upon Jesus' resurrection, Jesus received an immortal body as a new creation (1 Corinthians 15:23; Colossians 1:13-23).

When a new Believer receives a new perfect, sinless immortal male functioning born again spirit, and the immortal female functioning soul still has to become transformed by becoming spiritually minded, emotionally stable, and having God's sanctioned beliefs; then harmony is back to the Garden of Eden relationship before the fall because then the immortal female functioning soul has a relationship with the new immortal male functioning born again spirit in the same class of royalty. The perfect, righteous, holy, sinless, humble, obedient immortal male functioning born again spirit does not need any more transforming work, but the immortal female functioning soul was not born again and must be spiritually transformed (Romans 12:2).

As he did with Jesus in the temptation in the wilderness, the devil will try to entice a Believer's mortal male functioning body's hunger for lust of the flesh and lusts of the eyes, while the Believer's immortal female functioning soul's hunger for knowledge, emotions, and beliefs stimuli brought to her by the mortal male functioning body's five senses. Deceptively, Satan during his offer of temptations will never disclose the bondage that results from satisfying the desires of the fallen mortal male functioning body and the fallen immortal female functioning soul.

Satan is not personally tempted by sex, drugs, alcohol, food, or pornography, as he does not have flesh like a human being. These temptations of the mortal male functioning body were designed by Satan to cause the immortal male functioning body and the immortal female functioning soul to remain in the bondage of sin and die in sin if not saved by Christ Jesus.

The devil is tempted by self-exaltation and pride, but not the lust of the flesh or the lust of the eyes. The mortal male functioning body is a beast that needs to be tamed through Christ's crucifixion; whereas, the devil is a superior spirit, an immortal being who just plays with the lower created mortal male functioning body as a man would play with a pet dog. Therefore, the devil is full of the deceptions of the pride of life and promotes idol worship, false images, dysfunctional personalities, fleshly bad habits, and disguises himself as an angel of light to entice the immortal female functioning soul with false religions and beliefs.

Both the man and woman are tempted by Satan and therefore are equally vulnerable to temptations to sin. It is not uncommon to find that young women in teenage gangs are just as aggressive or more aggressive than the young men. Sometimes, it is the young woman who are the more rebellious teenager. Oftentimes, the most aggressive, competitive professionals in an industry are the women in the professions. Accordingly, one cannot say that either the man or woman as a whole person is the more sinful, prideful, aggressive, or rebellious. The reason is that men and women have both male and female characteristics needing to be redeemed and disciplined. There are differences physically between men and women bodies in the natural world, but these differences do not affect their authority, right, stature, mental agility, or hunger for authority and power in their immortal female functioning souls.

The devil became the administrator of a cursed planet. The devil usurped authority from Adam and Eve that Adam and Eve received from God over all the kingdoms of the world (Luke 4:5-6).

The devil has already been judged (John 12:31; 14:30; 16:11). Although the devil is not omnipresent, he does walk about the earth "...like a roaring lion, seeking whom he may devour" (1 Peter 5:8). In fact, the entire world lies under the sway of the devil (1 John 5:19). The devil, who is called the god of this world, has blinded the minds of those who are perishing from the truth of the gospel of the glory of Christ Jesus (2 Corinthians 4:4). He also has authority over the air and is called the prince of the power of the air (Ephesians 2:2). The devil rules with his kingdom of darkness over those who are not saved, both men and women; but Christ has destroyed the works of headship of the devil, and Jesus sits at the right hand of God in judgment over all principalities, powers, might, dominion, the rulers of the darkness of this age, and against spiritual hosts of wickedness in the heavenly places (Ephesians 1:20,21; 6:12; 1 John 3:8).

Likewise, the Believers, both men and women, are Kingdom Soldiers, and Believers' job is to resist the devil and he will flee (James 4:7). Believers are seated in Christ Jesus in heavenly places (Ephesians 2:6) and is also placed in authority through the headship of Christ Jesus above these evil powers (Ephesians 1:21-23).

God held both Adam and Eve equally responsible for committing sin in that they have equality in the fallen state of all mankind. Men are not more fallen than women; they both are equally fallen creatures before God. Likewise, both men and women are given the same punishment upon death of infernal damnation if they do not accept Jesus Christ as Lord and Savior. Thus men are not better or worse than women spiritually.

The Man and Woman are equals when they become born again

Chapter Four

CHAPTER FOUR

The Man and Woman Are Equals When They Become Born Again

To Nicodemus, Jesus said: "Verily, verily I say unto thee, except a man (and woman) be born again, he (and she) cannot see the Kingdom of God" (John 3:3). When a man and woman are truly saved, they immediately received a born again spirit, not a born again soul. Thus, if you are saved, your born again spirit is perfect, sinless, righteous, and holy (Hebrews 12:23; 1 John 3:9; Ephesians 4:24); but your soul is in a need of being spiritually transformed into the image and likeness of Christ (Romans 12:2).

Ephesians 2:1 says, "And you (both man and woman) hath He quickened (made alive) who were dead (nekros-corpse spiritually) in trespasses (paraptoma- faults) and sins (hamartia - offenses)." It was the immortal male functioning spirits of both men and women who were dead or unregenerate and not functioning in hearing God's voice prior to being born again. The immortal female functioning souls were being fed the sensory knowledge from the mortal male functioning body living in the world trying to make decisions about life with the reasoning of a fallen mind, the expressing of fallen emotions, based upon false beliefs, derived from the false teachers and the temporary stimuli received from this fallen four-dimensional world under the rulership of the fallen prince of this world.

What made the immortal female functioning soul respond when God pursued her for salvation? Was the void or vacuum still inside after each temporal stimuli experience from this four-dimensional world?

Scripture makes it clear that God first sought out a Believer's immortal female functioning soul, as the Believer's immortal female functioning soul knew there just had to be more to life than watching the mortal male functioning body eating, drinking, sleeping, fornicating, and acquiring possessions, the stimulus which continued to result in dissatisfaction and emptiness.

Ephesians 2:8-9 continues: "For by grace (unmerited favor and the Holy Spirit's power-word of operational means) are ye saved through faith; and that not of yourselves, it is the gift of God: not of works, lest any man should boast." You cannot save yourself, no matter how good you try to be. All people need Christ Jesus as the final Mediator between God and mankind.

Romans 10:9 says, "That if thou shalt confess with thy mouth the Lord Jesus, and shalt believe in thine heart that God hath raised Him from the dead, thou shalt be saved." Confessing with the mouth and believing in the heart are all immortal female functioning soul instigated actions by the mortal male functioning body and the heart in the immortal female functioning soul. The immortal female functioning soul must be genuinely repentant in the heart, with sincerity, decides with her free will to accept Jesus as Savior and Lord. Salvation does not come with just a mental ascent or an emotional high as salvation is a change of belief in a Believer's heart along with a heartfelt confession that Jesus is Lord.

Jesus not only defeated the works of the devil by destroying the devil's usurped headship possessory authority over the earth (1 John 3:8), but Jesus' death and resurrection gave eternal life to Believers' immortal female functioning soul. At the same time Jesus' incorruptible Seed planted inside Believers gave birth to Believers' new immortal male functioning born again spirit. In the resurrection, Believers will be given a new immortal male functioning spiritual body (1 Corinthians 15:23, 51-52).

The immortal male functioning born again spirit is a new creature, new man in Christ, who is perfectly holy and righteous (John 3:3; 2 Corinthians 5:17; 1 Peter 1:23; Hebrews 12:23; 1 John 3:9; Ephesians 4:24). After receiving a new immortal male functioning born again spirit, Believers have all the benefits, whether man or woman, associated with being reconciled with the Godhead (2 Corinthians 5:18).

After receiving the new immortal male functioning born again spirit, the Godhead moved inside Believers' mortal male functioning body and established His holy Temple. [1 Corinthians 3:16 (local Church); 2 Corinthians 6:16 (individually); and Ephesians 2:21 (universal Church)]. Additionally, after receiving the new immortal male functioning born again spirit, Believers became citizens of heaven (Philippians 3:20), Christ's Kingdom Ambassadors (2 Corinthians 5:20), Christ's Kingdom Soldiers (2 Timothy 2:3-4), Kings, lords, and priests (1 Timothy 6:15; Revelation 1:6), as spiritual vocations. Since men and women Believers receive the same spiritual benefits upon salvation, how can any religious Believer leader say that women are disqualified to be Pastors or the other Ephesians 4:11 Ministers.

After the immortal female functioning soul's sincere confession of faith, the immortal female functioning soul may not feel she is saved or even may doubt she is saved, but being saved is not a mental ascent or emotional high. The immortal female functioning soul's assurance that she is saved is that God is not a man that lies (Numbers 23:19), and He is certainly not like the devil who is the father of lies (John 8:44). God is a covenant making and covenant keeping almighty God, all loving, all knowing, and now always will be present intimately inside of the mortal male functioning body. God seeks intimacy with the immortal male functioning born again spirit and the immortal female functioning soul that is being transformed daily by the entire Godhead.

The reason the immortal female functioning soul may not feel she is saved or even doubt her salvation is because she is still carnally minded and not spiritually minded. The immortal female functioning soul is not instantly new or transformed from carnality to spirituality or from sin to righteousness and holiness because God did not want to wipe out her memory or personality. Transformation of the immortal female functioning soul is an arduous and tenacious process of ridding the influence of the flesh out of the receptive immortal female functioning soul, who still craves daily stimuli. Thus, the Holy Spirit sends the immortal male functioning born again spirit with the word of God to sow the word of God's Kingdom in the heart of the immortal female functioning soul (Matthew 13:19), as the rhema words of Jesus are spirit and life (John 6:63).

At first, the new Believer is enamored by these new spiritual words of the Kingdom that are very loving, new, positive, and very satisfying to the immortal female functioning soul. Since she is receptive, the immortal female functioning soul invites more and more spiritual words and an intimate relationship started developing between the Godhead and the immortal male functioning born again spirit with the immortal female functioning soul.

Sometimes, the word of God's Kingdom is soothing, loving, affirmative; and other times the word of God's Kingdom confronts sins, bad thinking, bad relationships, and false religious beliefs. As the Betrothed of Christ, the immortal female functioning soul learns that the blessing of Christ will be a marriage that lasts for all eternity.

Therefore, be anxious for nothing (Philippians 4:6). God will not give the immortal female functioning soul an evil spirit of fear, but of power, love, and a sound mind (2 Timothy 1:7). The immortal female functioning soul will discover that God is love personified (1 John 4:8); and that "Nor height, nor depth, nor any other creature, shall be able to separate us from the love of God, which is in Christ Jesus our Lord" (Romans 8:39).

Eventually, the immortal female functioning soul comes to the place of transformation and has tremendous faith because of hearing continuously the rhema word of God that engenders faith (Romans 10:17). The immortal female functioning soul is in the Kingdom of God where there is righteousness, peace, and joy in the Holy Spirit (Romans 14:17), as the Kingdom of God is what she daily seeks (Matthew 6:33). Then the immortal female functioning soul believes fervently in the heart that she knows "... that all things work together for good to them that love God, to them who are the called according to His purpose" (Romans 8:28).

The most important scripture that the immortal female functioning soul needs to put into practice and submit to transformation is Galatians 2:20, which says, "I am crucified with Christ: nevertheless I live; yet not I, but Christ liveth in me: and the life which I now live in the flesh I live by the faith of the Son of God, who loved me, and gave Himself for me."

The immortal female functioning soul knows that a Believer does not have to die an infernal death. Jesus said in John 11:25-26, "I am the resurrection, and the life: he that believeth in Me, though he were dead, yet shall he live: And whosoever liveth and believeth in Me shall never die. Believest thou this?"

The immortal female functioning soul receives and accepts zoe life forevermore, but the better news is while here on earth with the immortal male functioning born again spirit and the entire Godhead living inside the mortal male functioning body, the immortal female functioning soul no longer has to do the living but can allow Christ's divine nature to live His zoe life through and in the immortal female functioning soul to minister to others by preaching the gospel of the kingdom and the repentance and remission of sins.

The more the immortal female functioning soul receives and accepts the presence of the Godhead, the stronger the anointing. To become a better servant in God's Kingdom, the immortal female functioning soul must become an effective love doulos servant of Christ in God's Kingdom. That is the goal for transforming the immortal female functioning soul. John 3:5-6 says, "Verily, verily, I say unto thee, 'Except a man be born of water and of the Spirit (of Christ's resurrected humanity nature), he cannot enter into the kingdom of God. (6) That which is born of the flesh is flesh; and that which is born of the Spirit (of Christ's resurrected humanity nature) is spirit."

How does God convince the immortal female functioning soul, with her mind, emotions, and heart to exercise the will spiritually, holy, and righteous, unto being transformed and matured as a faithful Minister servant of Christ as King in God's Kingdom. The process of soul transformation, as mandated by Romans 12:2 is through renewal and transformation, which comes incrementally by God the Father pruning away the influence of the flesh in the immortal female functioning soul to bear more spiritual fruit (John 15:2), God the Word washing away the dirty flesh and sanctifying the immortal female functioning soul by the rhema word of God (Ephesians 5:26), and God the Holy Spirit mortifying the deeds of the flesh in the immortal female functioning soul to substitute more zoe life (Romans 8:13).

The immortal female functioning soul exercises her will to be renewed and transformed because she wants to be Godly and not carnal in her mind, emotions, and heart. At first, the immortal female functioning soul still wants to stay in control, as she notices that the immortal male functioning born again spirit and the entire Godhead living inside the mortal male functioning body do not want to be dictators but wants to lovingly transform the immortal female functioning soul spiritually instead of carnally. The immortal male functioning born again spirit and the Godhead want the immortal female functioning soul to experience God's presence in His spiritual Kingdom, expressing His agape love and Christ's resurrected zoe life, which personifies the new man in the immortal female functioning soul's life. The immortal female functioning soul is content finally, as she has found the life and love of God and Christ, and her purpose of becoming a child of God and servant in God's Kingdom here on earth as it is in heaven during this season and time has become spiritual reality.

Romans 7:6 says, "But now we are delivered from the law, that being dead wherein we were held; that we should serve in newness of spirit, and not in the oldness of the letter." The Law was the strength of sin (1 Corinthians 15:56), but Christ's grace and love is the strength of Believers' new resurrected lives in Believers' immortal male functioning born again spirits.

Romans 2:29 states, "But he is a Jew who is one inwardly; and circumcision is that of the heart in the spirit (as opposed to the heart being under the influence of the flesh), not in the letter; whose praise is not from men but from God." Both men and women can have circumcision of the heart where their wills reside in the receptive immortal female functioning soul when the immortal male functioning born again spirit comes into the heart, sows the seed of the word of the Kingdom (Matthew 13:19), to start the spiritual growth to transform and satisfy the desires of the heart in the immortal female functioning soul.

On the other hand, in the natural under Jewish Law only the men would bear circumcision as a sign of the Abrahamic Covenant. The heart in the immortal female functioning soul must become spiritual; so, that the will is led by the immortal male functioning born again spirit under the leading of the Holy Spirit and not by the pressures, temptations, and lusts of the mortal male functioning body. Those whose wills are led by the Spirit of God are the children of God (Romans 8:14-17). The Israelites of the Old Testament were God's chosen people from whom the Messiah came. However, the blessing of all people, both Jews and Gentiles, comes through Abraham through the Promise that was through the birth of Isaac, and then Jacob, and then the tribe of Judah, and the family of David and finally the Messiah, Christ Jesus. Galatians 3:16 says, "Now to Abraham and his Seed were the promises made. He saith not, 'And to seeds, as of many; but as of One, And to Thy Seed, which is Christ."

God called and chose those in the New Testament Ekklesia, both men and women, before the foundation of the world to be born again Believers. Ephesians 1:4-5 reveals this eternal truth: "According as He hath chosen us (men and women) in Him before the foundation of the world, that we (men and women) should be holy and without blame before Him in love: (5) Having predestinated us unto the adoption of children by Jesus Christ to Himself, according to the good pleasure of His will." That which is holy and without blame is a reference to Believers' new, immortal male functioning born again spirits with their new zoe resurrection life of Christ's resurrected humanity nature, who is the immortal male functioning born again spirit's spiritual DNA everlasting Father (Isaiah 9:6); and we are Father God's children by way of adoption (Romans 8:15).

Romans 6:13 commands, "Neither yield ye your members as instruments of unrighteousness unto sin: but yield yourselves unto God, as those that are alive from the dead, and your members as instruments of righteousness unto God." Paul clarifies that the true essence of Believers, both men and women, as Christ's new Second Man are "alive from the dead," which describes Believers' new, immortal male functioning born again spirits living with the indwelling entire Godhead in the body of the Believer which is the Temple of God.

In 2 Corinthians 5:17 Paul proclaims the most fundamental truth for men and women Believers: "Therefore, if anyone (both male and female, Greek or Jew, slave or free) is in Christ, he (generic Believer) is a new creation (a new spiritual species); old things have passed away; behold, all things have become new." After the initial salvation experience, Believers still had many old thoughts, emotional outbursts, and memories, whether man or woman in their immortal female functioning souls. Believers probably wondered, "How can we be saved and still have these same old thoughts and emotional outburst?"

Did Believers' immortal female functioning souls become born again and become new creatures in Christ as the Second Man? If so, then all old thoughts and sinful fleshly habits would have passed away if Believers' immortal female functioning souls were immediately born again. If that was the truth, then Believers' immortal female functioning souls would have no memories, no habits of bad emotional responses, no physical addictions, no problems with lust of the eyes, no problems with lust of the flesh, and no problems with pride of life. Yet, that is not the case.

Unlike Believers new immortal male functioning born again spirits, Believers' immortal female functioning souls were not transformed immediately unto perfection because Believers' souls still seek stimuli from the mortal male functioning body, from the kingdom of darkness, and from the fallen world system that is producing fallen stimuli in the form of sounds, sights, taste, touch, and smell through the body's five senses.

Unfortunately, the current world system is dominated by the devil (John 17:14-16; 15:19); so, Believers are in this fallen world, but are not of this fallen world, as Believers are citizens of heaven (Philippians 3:20). Believers are Christ's Kingdom spiritual Ambassadors (2 Corinthians 5:20), Christ's Kingdom spiritual Soldiers (2 Timothy 2:3-4), and Kings, lords, and priests (1 Timothy 6:15; Revelation 1:6).

Believers' immortal male functioning born again spirits were perfectly created without any sin (Hebrews 12:23; 1 John 3:9). As the prophesized Messiah, Jesus is Believers' spiritual DNA everlasting Father (Isaiah 9:6; Hebrews 2:13). Believers' immortal male functioning born again spirits are joined with the Spirit of Christ's resurrected humanity nature as one spirit (1 Corinthians 6:17). Believers' immortal male functioning born again spirits do not sin after salvation (1 John 3:9). Believers' immortal male functioning born again spirits are righteous and holy before God and mankind here on earth (Ephesians 4:24).

The changing of the priesthood to Melchizedek: John the Baptist, of the tribe of Levi, was a Priest under the old covenant; and during the baptism of Jesus, John the Baptist officiated the changing of the priesthood from the old order of the Levites and Aaron Priesthood to a new higher priestly order, the order of Melchizedek (Hebrews Chp.7). In recognition of John the Baptist's participation of changing the priesthood, Matthew 11: 11 says, "Verily I say unto you, 'Among them that are born of women there hath not risen a greater than John the Baptist: notwithstanding he that is least in the kingdom of heaven is greater than he."

Speaking of the Messiah, David said in Psalms 110:4, "The LORD hath sworn, and will not repent, 'Thou art a Priest forever after the order of Melchizedek.'" Melchizedek was not only a Priest but also was the King of Salem. Hebrews 7:1 says, "For this Melchizedek, King of Salem, Priest of the Most High God, who met Abraham returning from the slaughter of the kings and blessed him." Thus, Believers are Jesus' under Kings, under Lords, and under Priests of the order of Melchizedek here on earth.

Speaking of Jesus as Believers' High Priest, Hebrews 3:1 says, "Wherefore, holy brethren, partakers of the heavenly calling, consider the Apostle and High Priest of our profession, Christ Jesus." 1 Timothy 6:15 says, "Which in His times He shall shew, Who (Jesus) is the blessed and only Potentate, the King of kings, and Lord of lords." All Believers, both men and women, are Jesus' under kings and lords here on earth, not only the men. Revelation 1:6 says, "And hath made us (Believers under) kings and priests unto God and His Father; to Him be glory and dominion forever and ever."

Believers, both men and women, are Priests of the order of the Melchizedek, not just men. 1 Peter 2: 5, 9 says, "Ye also as lively stones, are built up a spiritual house, an holy priesthood, to offer up spiritual sacrifices, acceptable to God by Jesus Christ...(9) But ye are a chosen generation, a royal priesthood (kings and priests), an holy nation, a peculiar people; that ye should shew forth the praises of him who hath called you out of darkness into his marvelous light."

In the spirit world, there is no distinction between male and female in the offices of kings, lords, and priests who have an immortal male functioning born again spirit that is perfectly submitted to the King of kings, the Lord of lords, and the Highest Priest of priests (Galatians 3:28; 1 Timothy 6:15; Revelation 1:6; 17:14; 18:16).

Unfortunately, Believers still have their old and damaged self-images in their immortal female functioning souls that Believers are still nurturing, protecting, maturing, satisfying, and trying to become spiritually transformed. These fractures in Believers' self-conscious immortal female functioning souls show up in their works, their ministries, their relationships with others, and their responses to the stresses of life.

Jesus' precious blood: All people who have ever lived, are living, and will ever live were in the loins of Adam in seed form when he committed high treason against God in the Garden of Eden (Romans 5:12). These Scriptures also refer to Believers' tickets unto everlasting life in Christ through the spilt blood of Jesus. Believers' old mortal male functioning spirit was not raised from the dead when new Believers heartfelt confession of faith accepted Jesus as their Lord and Savior. Believers received a sinless, righteous, holy, perfect, new immortal male functioning born again spirit that has resurrected zoe life and does not sin (Ephesians 4:24; 1 Peter 1:23; Hebrews 12:23; 1 John 3:9). 1 Peter 1:23 says, "Being born again, not of corruptible seed, but of incorruptible, by the word of God, which liveth and abideth forever."

1 Peter 1:18-19 says, "Forasmuch as ye know that ye were not redeemed with corruptible things, as silver and gold, from your vane conversation receive by tradition from your fathers; (19) But with the precious blood of Christ, as of a lamb without blemish and without spot." The blood of Jesus did a perfect work to both the man and woman alike to bring forth their new perfect immortal male functioning born again spirits by the incorruptible seed of Christ's resurrected humanity nature.

Just like the men Believers, women Believers receive the same born-again spirit and become the same new creatures in Christ, so how can women Believers be disqualified to be Ephesians 4:11 Ministers?

Jesus' blood that redeemed both woman and man Believers is precious and perfect. A woman Believer's new immortal male functioning born again spirit came from Jesus' resurrected incorruptible seed as the spiritual DNA everlasting Father (Isaiah 9:6; Hebrews 2:13), the same as men. This new immortal male functioning born again spirit creature is perfect, righteous, holy, and does not sin (1 Peter 1:23; Hebrews 12:23; Ephesians 4:24; 1 John 3:9).

Then, on what basis is a woman Believer, with her new spiritual immortal male functioning born again spirit the same as a man Believer that is perfect, righteous holy, does not sin, and this woman Believer's body is the Temple of the Godhead inside of her (1 Corinthians 3:16; 2 Corinthians 6:16; Ephesians 2:21), is disqualified from functioning as an apostle, prophet, evangelist, pastor, or teacher? This means that the arguments against women Ephesians 4:11 Ministers are mere traditions of man and not the restrictions brought by Father God, God the Word, God's Son King, and God the Holy Spirit.

Women and men Believers are both born again and saved not as the result of works, "lest any man should boast" (Ephesians 2:9). Believers do not earn by good works the new immortal male functioning born again spirit or salvation experience. Women and men Believers' entire beings receive vicariously the gift of eternal life immediately upon accepting Jesus Christ as Savior and Lord in their hearts.

Notwithstanding, both men and women Believers do not immediately experience the full transformation or sanctification of their immortal female functioning souls. It is also the blessing of Believers when they receive a new immortal male functioning spiritual body in the future (1 Corinthians 15:23) that will be needed when Believers return to earth to rule and reign with Jesus when there is a new heaven and new earth (Revelation chp.21). There are no distinctions between men and women regarding their eternal blessing of being born again or having the right to receive a new immortal male functioning spiritual body in the future. Where in these truths from scripture disqualify women from being Ephesians 4:11 Ministers?

Again, Hebrews 12:23 addresses men and women Believers having perfected immortal male functioning born again spirits: ". . . And to the spirits (pnuema) of just (dikaios- innocent, holy) men (generic for both male and female) made perfect (teleioo -complete, totally mature, finished, flawless character)." A man and woman Believer can aid in the maturing of the Believer's immortal female functioning soul because she was created to make free-will choices and can choose to submit to the Godhead. However, only God can make something or someone into a new perfect creature in Christ (1 Corinthians 15:47; 2 Corinthians 5:17).

Both men and women were fallen spiritual beings, and they equally have no power to fix themselves. God's original created man and woman had death implanted in them both because of eating the forbidden fruit. God the Creator could not just repair, fix, or forgive the old sinful man and woman. God had to cause fallen man and woman to have new immortal male functioning born again sprits as the new creation in Christ, a new species of man and woman, birthed from the resurrected incorruptible Seed of the humanity nature of Christ Jesus, the Second Man, (2 Corinthians 5:17; 1 Corinthians 15:47; 1 Peter 1:23).

Healing by His stripes, along with renewal, renovation, salvation, and forgiveness for remission of sins required a perfect sinless Man as a Sacrificial Lamb of God (Christ Jesus), born without sin, committing no sin (2 Corinthians 5:21; Hebrews 4:15; 1 Peter 2:22-23), but voluntarily dying on a Roman Cross for the sins of fallen men and women alike, and to be justifiably raised from the dead with resurrection life. From His resurrected Spirit, Christ Jesus passes His Seed to every Believer to give birth to the immortal male functioning born again spirit. Only the Son of God, the Sinless Lamb being sacrificed for sinful fallen men and women could satisfy Father God's sense of justice. Since God chose to forgive, save, and grant women a new male functioning born again spirit from Jesus' resurrected Spirit, how can this disqualify women from being Ministers in God's Kingdom?

Men and women's redemption included an identification with Jesus' humanity nature's resurrection life and the stature of the humanity nature of Jesus as the Second Man. Jesus' humanity nature was tested and tempted in all things yet did not sin (Hebrews 4:15). He passed the test with a perfect score because he learned obedience by the things His humanity nature suffered (Hebrews 5:8). Hebrews 5:9 declares of Jesus: "And having been perfected, He became the Author of eternal salvation to all who obey Him." Since women received the same eternal salvation as the men, on what grounds are men given the authority to disqualify women from ministry?

When new men and women Believers accept Jesus Christ as Savior and Lord, they both are joined with Christ as one spirit (1 Corinthians 6:17). Jesus Christ humanity nature's resurrected spirit is the firstborn of many brethren (generic for man and woman) from the dead (Colossians 1:18). When men and women Believers were joined in spirit with Christ, they both received in their new immortal male functioning born again spirits perfection, righteousness, and holiness (Ephesians 4:24; Hebrews 12:23). Christ Jesus imparted His perfection, sinlessness, righteousness, and holiness into both man and woman Believers' new immortal male functioning born again spirits by the implantation of Jesus' holy and incorruptible Seed (1 Peter 1:23). God did not make junk, and Christ gave both women and men His best in full maturity form, which was a free gift at initial salvation. This gift did not make a man Believer superior to a woman Believer, so why are women treated unequally in some denominations.

Colossians 1:22 says, "Yet, He has now reconciled you (both men and women) in His fleshly (sarx) body (soma) through death, in order to present you (both men and women) before Him holy (hagios- sacred, pure, consecrated) and blameless (anomos - without blame, spot, blemish or fault) and beyond reproach (anegklitos - unaccused, irreproachable, unreproveable, without sin)." That part of Believers (both men and women) that is "holy and blameless and beyond reproach" is both men and women Believers' immortal male functioning born again spirits.

There is no spiritual distinction between men and women in this Scripture (Galatians 3:28). That part of the Believer that is "holy and blameless and beyond reproach" is the men and women Believers' new immortal male functioning born again spirits; not their immortal female functioning souls.

Ephesians 2:5-6, 10 declares: "Even when we (men and women) were dead in our trespasses, made us alive together with Christ (by grace you have been saved), and raised us with Him in the heavenly places, in Christ Jesus. . . For we (men and women) are his workmanship, created in Christ Jesus unto good works, which God hath before ordained that we should walk in them."

Both men and women Believers must submit to accept the death process by entering the crucifixion of Christ that mortifies the passions and carnal desires of the flesh's influence in both men and women Believers' immortal female functioning souls and inviting Christ to live His resurrected life in them and through them to minister to others (Romans 6:6; Galatians 2:20; 5:24).

Colossians 3: 9-10 says, "...Seeing that ye have put off the old man (flesh) with his deeds; and (10), have put on the New Man (immortal male functioning born again spirit) which is renewed in knowledge after the image of Him that created him: (11) Where there is neither Greek nor Jew, circumcision nor uncircumcision, Barbarian, Scythian, bond nor free: but Christ is all, and in all (both men and women)."

2 Timothy 4:22 says, "The Lord Jesus Christ be with your spirit...." Here, the immortal male functioning born again spirit, being male in function in both men and women, so how does this scripture disqualify women from being Ephesians 4:11 Ministers?

The reference in these Scriptures is directed to immortal male functioning born again spirits of both men and women Believers (1 Peter 1:23). The resurrected Jesus as Messiah is both men and women Believers' spiritual DNA everlasting Father of their immortal male functioning born again spirits (Isaiah 9:6; Hebrews 2:13).

It should be noted that in the Greek there is no distinction between lowercase letters and uppercase letters. Therefore, scholars differ, for example, when the word spirit is used in scripture. The Greek word for spirit is pneuma. Thus, some scholars interpret pneuma meaning the flesh versus the spirit, God the Holy Spirit, the spirit of Christ, or the born-again spirit of Believers. Now, let's look at some scriptures that are revealing.

Ephesians 2:6 says, "And hath raised us (Believers immortal male functioning born again spirit) up together and made us (Believers immortal male functioning born again spirit) sit together in heavenly places in Christ Jesus." Men and women Believers have immortal male functioning born again spirits which are intimately in fellowship in Christ Jesus as if they are one, like a close child is with his or her father.

Romans 8:9-10 says, "But ye (immortal female functioning soul) are not in the flesh, but in the spirit (flesh versus spirit), if so be that the Spirit of God (Holy Spirit) dwell in you. Now if any man have not the Spirit of Christ (referring to Christ's resurrected humanity nature Spirit joined with a Believer's immortal male functioning born again spirit), he is none of His. (10) And if Christ be in you (referring to Christ's resurrected humanity nature Spirit joined with a Believer's immortal male functioning born again spirit), the body is dead because of sin; but the spirit (Believer's male functioning born again spirit) is life because of righteousness (Ephesians 4:24; Colossians 1:22; 3:10).

2 Corinthians 3:17 says, "Now the Lord is that spirit: and where the spirit of the Lord is, there is liberty." Here is a reference representing the spirit of the resurrected humanity nature of the Lord Jesus Christ, not His divine nature, God the Word, and not the Holy Spirit. If a man or woman does not have an immortal male functioning born again spirit, the man or woman cannot experience the liberty that the Lord wants both men and women Believers to have because 1 Corinthians 6:17 says, "But he that is joined unto the Lord is one spirit." It is your immortal male functioning born again spirit that is joined to the Lord that allows you the liberty that is in Christ's resurrected humanity nature spirit. If a man or woman Believer is saved, it is because the man or woman Believer was chosen to be in Christ before the foundation of the world (Ephesians 1:4-5). Yet, to be clear, God is all knowing, not all controlling, as God's creative design gave men and women free will to make choices, and the Believer must have a heart cry that calls upon the name of the Lord to be redeemed. God just knows who is going to call on the name of the Lord.

For example, Adam and Eve sinned by eating the forbidden fruit, but their sin did not catch God by surprise because He is all knowing. God knew they would sin, and God had a Redeemer in His bosom, the only begotten Son of God, the Messiah, and Christ who in the fullness of time God planned beforehand to send Him to earth to redeem man and to inaugurate His kingdom again here on earth (Matthew 4:17; 6:10).

Galatians 4: 4-5 says, "But when the fulness of the time was come, God sent forth his Son, made of a woman, made under the law, (5) To redeem them that were under the law, that we might receive the adoption of sons."

God wants both men and women Believers' perfect, mature, holy, and righteous immortal male functioning born again spirits to follow the leading of the Holy Spirit to illuminate a Believer's heart by sowing a seed that is the word of the Kingdom (Matthew 13:19) where the library of beliefs is stored. The heart is also where the will resides in the man and woman Believer's immortal female functioning soul to transform her to be spiritual and no longer carnal. This must be done in both men and women. Why does this tough cleansing have to be done to women the same as men if the women are disqualified to be leaders in the body of Christ, and not qualified to be an Ephesians 4:11 office gift Minister?

Referring to both men and women, the scriptures state in God's point of view men and women Believers are primarily sons because both men and women have new immortal male functioning born again spirits. Galatians 4:6-7 says, "And because ye are sons (immortal male functioning born again spirits by adoption), God hath sent forth the (resurrected humanity) spirit of His Son into your hearts, crying, Abba, Father. (7) Wherefore thou art no more a servant, but a son; and if a son, then an heir of God through Christ." The word spirit is a reference to Christ's resurrected spirit of His humanity nature that is joined with the Believer's immortal female functioning soul. Since they joined together as one spirit (1 Corinthians 6:17), then when men and women Believers' born again spirits enter the heart, the men and women's immortal male functioning born again spirits are joined with Christ's resurrected humanity spirit and together plant the word of the Kingdom into the heart.

Romans 8:15-16 reveals, "For ye (both men and women) have not received the spirit of bondage again to fear; but ye have received the spirit of adoption, whereby we cry, Abba, Father. (16) The Spirit (Holy Spirit) itself beareth witness with our spirit (immortal male functioning born again spirit), that we are the children of God." Again, the spiritual DNA Father of our immortal male functioning born again spirits is Christ Jesus resurrected humanity nature (Isaiah 9:6; 1 Corinthians 1:23; Hebrews 2:13).

Speaking about women's immortal male functioning born again spirits, 1 Peter 3:3-4 says, "Whose adorning let it not be that outward adorning of plaiting the hair and wearing of gold or putting on of apparel. But let it be the hidden man (immortal male functioning born again spirit coming into) the heart (the gateway into the soul), in that which is not corruptible (immortal male functioning born again spirit), even the ornament of a meek and quiet (immortal male functioning born again) spirit, which is in the sight of God of great price."

The "meek and quiet (immortal male functioning born again) spirit" in both men and women has great value with God because the immortal male functioning born again spirit is joined with the resurrected humanity Spirit of Christ Jesus who is the spiritual DNA everlasting Father (1 Corinthians 6:17; Isaiah 9:6) through the omnipresence of God the Word, Jesus' divine nature.

It deserves repeating that Christ Jesus' divine nature is God the Word that is inseverable, distinguishable, and separable from Jesus' humanity nature. God the Word was made flesh (John 1:14), and Jesus' resurrected humanity nature personified is the spiritual DNA everlasting Father of Believers' immortal male functioning born again perfect spirits (Isaiah 9:6; Hebrews 2:13). Matthew 11:27 says, "All things are delivered unto me of My Father: and no man knoweth the Son, but the Father; neither knoweth any man the Father, save the Son, and he to whomsoever the Son will reveal Him." Therefore, besides God the Father, God the Word, and God the Holy Spirit, Jesus' resurrected humanity nature is the only one qualified to explain God to man and Who best reveals that He is the spiritual DNA everlasting Father of Believers' immortal male functioning born again perfect spirit.

2 Timothy 1:9 says, "Who (God) hath saved us (both men and women) and called us (both men and women) with a holy calling, not according to our works, but according to His own purpose and grace, which were given us (both men and women) in Christ Jesus before the world began."

If women, the same as men, were called by God with a holy calling and according to God's own purpose and grace "before the world began" why do some men Believers as Church leaders do not recognize God's calling of women into ministry as Ephesian 4:11 Ministers?

The rhema spoken word, communicated by the Holy Spirit to Believers' immortal male functioning born again spirits is what comes into Believers' hearts from the spiritual realm to bring the experiential spiritual reality of salvation and sanctification to heal, to transform, to sanctify, to make wise unto salvation, and to spiritually mature Believers' immortal female functioning souls.

Experiential reality of salvation is the present-day manifestation of living in the Kingdom of God with His blessings but is merely a foretaste (Hebrews 6:5) of things to come but leading to the everlasting life in heaven for a season and the return to earth to rule and reign with Christ forever (Revelation 5:10). This is the present and future hope for both men and women. Men and women are kings and priests who will rule with Christ forever (Revelation 5:10). Thus, why would men in religious leadership say that women Believers are disqualified to be kings and priests now since men Believers affirm falsely, they, but not women, are only the kings and priests now and forever with Christ.

The new immortal male functioning born again spirit has been birthed into royalty in Christ Jesus. Revelations 1:5-6 reveals: ". . . To Him who loved us and washed us from our sins in His own blood and has made us (both men and women) kings and priests to His God and Father, to Him be glory and dominion forever and ever. Amen." Thus, why are not women recognized as God's kings and priests now? Was Christ's precious blood that washed men and women clean from their sins somehow elevated and honored only men Believers to be kings and priests but did not elevate and honored women to be kings and priests?

Likewise, 1 Peter 2:9 says, "But you (men and women) are a chosen generation, a royal priesthood, a holy nation, his own special people, that you may proclaim the praises of Him who called you out of darkness into His marvelous light." If God chose both men and women to be a chosen generation, a royal priesthood, a holy nation, His own special people, then how can religious men leaders reject God's choices to substitute man's choices?

As a chosen generation, a royal priesthood, a holy nation, God's own special people, the new immortal male functioning born again spirit of both men and women have been bestowed with delegated exousia authority from Christ Jesus to extend and administrate the dunamis power from, and being led by, the Holy Spirit to preach and spread the gospel of the Kingdom of God (Mathew 24:14) and repentance and remission of sins (Luke 24:47), and to share God's love to Believers' fellow humanity in the area of influence given to Believers as their kratos territorial dominion authority.

Men Believers who are leaders that treat women Believers as leaders with the same authority, spiritual anointing, and leadership positions of Ministry the same as men without discrimination are recognized as having right standing in the Kingdom of God.

By denying women their place in leadership, then the men leaders in Ministry that formed the rules and regulations of their denomination disqualifying women Believers from ministry, have been aiding and abetting the devil by taking away about 55% of the Kingdom Ambassadors and Kingdom Soldiers of Christ in the Church.

Jesus answered the religious Jewish leaders in Matthew 15:3, "...Why do ye also transgress the commandment of God by your tradition?" Psalms 78:41 "Yea, they turned back and tempted God, and limited the Holy One of Israel." Do men Believers espouse religious tradition instead of the leading of the Holy Spirit without realizing they are limiting the Holy Spirit that wants to accept volunteer women Believers as kings, lords, priests, Ambassadors, Soldiers, Servants, and Ephesian 4:11 Ministers in the Kingdom of God?

The Lord's admonishment is clear: Psalms 105:15, "Saying, 'Touch not mine anointed, and do my prophets no harm.'" How many anointed women, with some women being prophets, have men leaders of religious tradition touched the anointed women's ministry calling by disqualifying them as Ephesian 4:11 Minsters?

Men Believers and Leaders, it is time to come out of your religious denominational slumber and hear the words of God. Women Ministers have awakened and will follow the leading of the Holy Spirit and not the words of religious tradition. Women Believers are called by God to be Ephesians 4:11 Ministers the same as the men Believers.

The false interpretation of I Corinthians 11:4-6

Chapter Five

CHAPTER FIVE

The False Interpretation of 1 Corinthians 11:4-6

Scripture is clear that New Testament women Believers were allowed to pray and prophesy and exercise other gifts of the Spirit in public as part of their Christ-centered faith. Let us examine the false interpretation and misapplication of 1 Corinthians 11:4-5. These false interpretations and misapplications have kept women in bondage in the New Testament Church for almost 1,900 years.

The Prophetess Anna, as an Old Testament Prophet, was given a recognized and sanctioned public ministry to prophesy long before Jesus as a babe was brought to the Jewish Temple (Luke 2:36-38). Anna delivered God's prophecy to the assembled crowd of men and women looking for the Messiah. Using her gift of prophecy, Anna taught others in the temple. Apparently, the temple allowed women to teach; whereas, under Jewish tradition the synagogue allowed only the men to teach.

In 1 Corinthians 11:4-6, Apostle Paul recognized that both men and women have the right to pray and prophesy. "Every man praying or prophesying, having his head covered, dishonoureth his head. (5) But every woman that prayeth or prophesieth with her head uncovered dishonoureth her head: for that is even all one as if she were shaven. (6) For if the woman be not covered, let her also be shorn: but if it be a shame for a woman to be shorn or shaven, let her be covered."

The scripture passage does not nullify women from being Ephesians 4:11 Ministers. It is clear in other Scripture references in both the Old and New Testaments that both men and women were endowed with the gift of prophecy. Consequently, both men and women were allowed to edify, exhort, and comfort other members in the church by prophesying (1 Corinthians 14:3, 31).

The fact that women would prophesy in the New Testament Church was and is a fulfillment of prophecy in Joel 2:28, which Peter cited in his sermon in Acts 2:17 on the day of Pentecost. If prophecy were not allowed of women, this prophecy in Joel 2:28 could not be fulfilled, "Your sons and daughters shall prophesy."

Likewise, if women without the indwelling Holy Spirit were allowed to function in the office of the prophet, even in the Old Testament dispensation, such as Anna, above, how much more should New Testament women be allowed and celebrated to function in the office of the prophet since they have born again spirits and the indwelling Holy Spirit? Likewise, if women are allowed to function in the office of the prophet, how can one exclude them in the other Ephesians 4:11 ministry offices?

What does headship mean? The Greek word for head is kephale which is the same Greek word for head in Ephesians 5:23, 25 which declares, "For the husband (aner) is head (kephale) of the wife (gune), as also Christ is Head (kephale) of the Ekklesia; and He is the Savior of the body. . . Husbands (aner) love your wives (gune), just as Christ also loved the Ekklesia and gave Himself for her."

Christ laid down His own life to bring forth His Betrothed in all her splendor. The Greek word for the word gave is paradidomi which means, "to entrust, transmit, commit fully, to bring forth." The meaning of the Greek word for head in this context is a person who constantly gives to the one submitting total support, provides for his or her every need, brings him or her to a higher esteem, and brings glory to the one who submits. One can easily see that the husband was to support, honor, and care for the wife as he would his own body. Thus, this passage in Scripture cannot be interpreted to subjugate women as a second-class citizen in the church.

The definition of the word head means source of life. The word head is sort of like the fountainhead as the source of life of a river. The woman came from the man in the beginning, and in that sense the man was therefore the woman's source of life. Christ is the Head of the Ekklesia (Ephesians 1:22-23), and He is the Betrothed's source of life. "He who has the Son has life" (1 John 5:12).

Therefore, the husband as headship must continue being the purveyor of Christ's spiritual source of life through his obedient submission to Christ for the wife, as the husband has the responsibility to lay down his life for his wife and family. The husband must give up his life and give the resurrected life within him (which must be Christ Jesus living in and through the immortal male functioning born again spirit) to care for and bring benefit to his wife (Galatians 2:20).

The man's marital headship was not given to him just because the male man was first created. If that were true, insects would have authority over mankind because they were created first. The marital headship comes into the relationship to nourish, protect, and cause growth in the natural family and the spiritual family of God. Colossians 2:19 says, "And not holding fast to the Head, from whom all the body, nourished and knit together by joints and ligaments, grows with the increase that is from God." Christ Jesus, as the Head of the Betrothed, the Ekklesia, gives life, nourishment, and growth. This is the pattern for the husband as the marital head must provide nourishment, and protection, and be the man of God that is led by the Holy Spirit in all that he does.

Being the marital headship is not, "Me Tarzan, you Jane so obey!" The headship position does not mean the husband is allowed to take dominion over the wife. Thus, as the marital headship, the husband's headship does not give him the right to be domineering over the wife. As in Genesis 1:26-28, God never said that the man was originally created to have dominion over another man or woman. Enslavement is against God's creative design and purpose. Man and woman were given dominion together over the things of the earth in the original creation order, not just the man.

The Greek gune means both woman and wife. Similarly, the word woman in 1 Corinthians 11:4-6 could have easily been translated as wife as the same Greek word gune is used to mean the woman or wife. Similarly, the word for man or husband is the same Greek word, which is aner.

Hence, a better translation is that the proscription here concerns a wife with her husband and should not have been a prohibition against women in general. The Greek word for submission is hupotasso, which means, "to arrange in an orderly manner, or the subordination in an honorable and Godly manner." Colossians 2:10 says, "And ye are complete in Him (Jesus), which is the head of all principality and power." Submission to a Godly headship does not bring weakness, inferiority, or enslavement, but fulfillment and completeness; so, life, Himself, as the Head can flow into your family and everyone in the family (John 14:6).

Paul's teaching concerning whether a woman's head should be covered when she prayed or prophesied was merely to bring order in the Corinthian Ekklesia, and the verse should not be interpreted as signifying men's general superiority over women's general inferiority in the spiritual kingdom of God.

The prostitutes in Corinth in those days went around without veils or with their heads uncovered. An acknowledged badge of independence from their husbands were the wives who walked around without a veil. Some Corinthian wives thought they should outwardly display their newly found liberty in the Christian Ekklesia from cultural prejudices and bondages by discarding the veil. The veil was an acknowledged sign of dependence on and orderly submission with honor of a wife to a husband in that culture at that time in line with God's redemptive Kingdom order and plan as originally pronounced in Genesis 3:16.

Putting on a veil after marriage in that Corinthian culture at that time was a token assent that her husband was her head, provider, and protector. It is sort of like putting on the wedding ring and taking the husband's sir name in wedding ceremonies today in our culture. At that time when the prostitutes, or those caught in adultery, were exposed, the heads of these women publicly would be shaven as a symbol of public scorn. As may have been already surmised, the male prostitutes did not undergo the same disgrace as the women, which again discloses the unequal treatment.

The temptation of the Corinthian wives was to carry their newly acquired freedoms too far, according to Paul, which could hurt the growth of the still infant Ekklesia. You allow babies less freedom because of their weakness and immaturity than teenagers. You also must watch the young ones closely as they play with others of their age; so, they do not hurt each other. Paul had this idea in mind in 1 Corinthians 8:9 when he said, "But take heed lest by any means this liberty of yours become a stumbling block to them that are weak."

Christianity brought a great and rapid elevation of womanhood, but in its administration and activation there were incidental disorders in the services and practices which were addressed by Paul to bring harmony in marriage and to remove the people's minds off the flesh and onto the Spirit.

The Jewish men at time of Jesus: It was not only the women who were chastised by Paul. In 1 Corinthians 11:4 Paul also chastised the men for praying and prophesying with a prayer shawl on their heads, again making a cultural correction. This verse disciplining the men was never to be interpreted to tell the men they could not pray or prophesy in public, or that they were somehow inferior to others in the body of Christ. Paul simply was admonishing the men not to pray and prophesy in a wrong way.

Jewish men would worship in the synagogues wearing a head covering, to indicate their unworthiness before God because of their fallen nature from Adam. Paul pointed out that this tradition was improper in the Christian Ekklesia because "There is therefore now no condemnation to them which are in Christ Jesus, who walk not after the flesh, but after the Spirit" (Romans 8:1).

Accordingly, the Jewish practice of wearing the head covering called the tallith (prayer shawl) was a contradiction to a born again man's new standing before God in Christ, as Christ is now his Head and Covering; so, he can go boldly before the Throne of Grace by the blood of Jesus (Hebrews 4:16; 10:19). This positional change is reflected in Paul's statement in 2 Corinthians 3:16, "Nevertheless when it shall turn to the Lord, the veil shall be taken away."

The man Believer with his head uncovered and the woman Believer with her head covered in the Greek and Asian Cultures also denoted at that time the Biblical redemptive Kingdom order and responsibility. This Kingdom order is reflected in the triune nature of the Godhead, God the Father, God the Word, and God the Holy Spirit. In the King James version, 1 John 5:7 says, "For there are three that bear record in heaven, the Father, the Word, and the Holy Ghost: and these three are one."

Although all members of the one Godhead are equal and complement each other in God's Kingdom, there is a redemptive Kingdom order of authority and communication. In the redemptive Kingdom order of authority and communication, God the Word is voluntarily subordinate in authority and communication to God the Father, and God the Holy Spirit is voluntarily subordinate in authority and communication to God the Word.

Likewise, Believers' immortal male functioning born again spirits are voluntarily subordinate in authority and communication to the Holy Spirit. The transformation process of the immortal female functioning soul is to make her voluntarily subordinate in Kingdom authority and communication to the immortal male functioning born again spirit to ensure the immortal female functioning soul is voluntarily submitted to minister with God's spiritual authority, calling, and anointing. Thus, if the man or woman Ministers a healing, a prophecy, a word of knowledge, a word of wisdom, or the activation of another Believer into ministry, the minister is following the divine authority and communication from God.

Kingdom faith and authority: Faith comes from hearing and hearing by the rhema word of God (Romans 10:17), and if a Believer Ministers without first hearing God's word and instructions, then the Believer will be laying empty hands upon empty heads, no healing will occur, and the so-called word of prophecy or word of wisdom will be simply soulish words without God's power and authority, even though God's covenant will was for healing. Each Believer must spend much closet time in prayer, in worship, and in studying the logos word of God to know the still small voice of the Holy Spirit coming into the Believer's immortal male functioning born again spirit, which then must be transmitted to the Believer's immortal female functioning soul before the Believer Ministers to someone. The Believer with submission and practice can mature as a minister.

The River of Life flows from the authoritative throne of God and the Lamb (Revelation 22:1); so, the Kingdom experiential eternal life finally comes into the immortal female functioning soul of both men and women by flowing from God's redemptive Kingdom authority of communication. This voluntary subordination by the immortal female functioning soul is perfectly consistent with the equality and identity of attributes of each person of the Godhead and must be accepted truth by both men and women as children of God. Therefore, even though God the Word and God the Holy Spirit are one and equal with God the Father, they are voluntarily subordinate in Kingdom authority communication to God the Father. The Kingdom order of authority and communication ensures that the zoe and rhema from God the Father properly flows to the immortal male functioning born again spirit and then to the immortal female functioning soul. Although there is loving submission in God's redemption Kingdom order, there is never abuse of authority.

Let us look at Scriptural support for this concept. Jesus, consisting of His divine nature as God the Word and His humanity nature as the Only Begotten Son of God, only speaks and does what He hears and sees Father God saying and doing (John 7:16-18). In John 14:10 Jesus said, "Do you not believe that I am in the

Father, and the Father in Me? The words (rhema) that I speak to you I do not speak on my own authority; but the Father who dwells in Me does the works." Hebrews 1:1-2 coveys God's method of communication: "God, who at sundry times and in divers manners spake in time past unto the fathers by the prophets, (2) Hath in these last days spoken unto us by his Son, whom he hath appointed heir of all things, by whom also He made the worlds."

John 16:13-14 speaks of the voluntary subornation to God the Word; "Howbeit when He, the Spirit of truth, is come, He will guide you (men and women) into all truth: for He shall not speak of Himself; but whatsoever He shall hear, that shall He speak: and He will shew you (men and women) things to come. (14) He shall glorify Me: for He shall receive of Mine and shall shew it unto you (men and women)." The Holy Spirit declares the words spoken by God the Word as rhema to the immortal male functioning born again spirit, who then communicates to the immortal female functioning soul to make her spiritual to be a spiritual communicator to other people with spirit and life (John 6:63; Romans 8:6).

Since the Day of Pentecost, the beginning of the Ekklesia Age, the Holy Spirit has jurisdictional authority here on earth (John 16:7-15). Yet, authority is given only when there is proper submission, which is another of God's principles. Your immortal male functioning born again spirit is given the authority as joint priests of your home (that is your entire being) because he is perfectly submitted to the Godhead and without sin (1 John 5:18) and with perfect faith to overcome the world (1 John 5:4).

Likewise, a wife is given authority in the home and God's kingdom on the condition she stays submitted to her husband in God's redemptive kingdom order of authority and communication. In other words, he who voluntarily lays down his life for others unselfishly based upon agape love with God's kingdom authority as a servant as he or she is ministering to bring spiritual life to others. The humble servant is promoted in God's Kingdom (Philippians 2:5-9).

Therefore, like the husband; the joint king, lord, and priest, the wife is the Queen of the home, has great authority there, but she shows respect to the husband and father when he speaks, and at the same time the husband shows great respect to the wife and mother when she speaks. Thus, the father should tell their children, "Listen and obey your mother." Likewise, the mother should tell their children, "Listen and obey your father." The father and mother should always show respect and honor to each other, especially when the children are present. The husband submits to his wife when she is exercising her jurisdictional authority, and the wife submits to her husband when he is exercising his jurisdictional authority. Honor is mandatory in God's Kingdom and must be in every household and family.

Children learn by seeing and hearing. If the parents are not seen and heard by the children as respectful to each other, the children usually won't respect and honor their own spouse when they marry in the future. Remember, children take in and learn more the first seven years of their lives that often is more than they learn the total of the rest of their lives. Through their five senses, children learn language, reading, writing, math, different animals, different vegetation, colors, foods to eat, table manners, how to respectfully address adults, relationship behavior, cleaning their rooms, and even how to work cell phones and computers. The children of Believers also learn about Jesus, praying, going to Ekklesia, the meanings of Christmas and Easter, going to school and earning good grades, the importance of distinguishing areas where they speak softly or loudly on the playground, how to swim, doing chores, how to read signs, the sky and earth, sitting in special safety seats, don't talk to strangers, and never leave the house without their parents.

Even though Believers are the Temple of God in the local Ekklesia (1 Corinthians 3:16), individually (2 Corinthians 6:16), and in the universal Ekklesia (Ephesians 2:21), God sees them as male and female, neither Greek nor Jew, neither slave nor free, but all at the same time are Christ's body and therefore are one with Him. Believers, both man and woman, are voluntarily subordinate and subject to the Head, Christ Jesus (Ephesians 1:22-23). All Believers, both men and women, should submit to the Head. Everyone in the body of Christ lives under submitted and subordinate authority. There are no Lone Rangers allowed in the Kingdom of God. All Believers, both men and women, are Kingdom Ambassadors of Christ, Kingdom Soldiers of Christ, Kingdom Lords, kings, and priests. God sees faith that pleases Him when His children, both men and women, are submitted to Him as the bondservants of Christ Jesus.

Moreover, in the Kingdom of God, although both the male and female Believers have equal standing in Christ as His body as far as ministry is concerned, the wife is subordinate to the husband in the supportive activities of the home in God's Kingdom order. This is based upon the relationship of husband and wife, which is patterned after the family in heaven. However, without the relationship of husband and wife, the reason for submission by women to men in general is absent, and aberrant. Women in general should not submit to the authority of men in general. Yet, women lawyers submit to a judge the same as men lawyers. Both men and women submit to authority of University professors. Both men and women submit to the authority of police officers. Submission is not enslavement. It shows respect and honor, and thereby they receive honor in return.

For example, the Lord has given as gifts certain men and women as delineated in Ephesians 4:11 who are apostles, prophets, evangelists, pastors and/or teachers. When Ministers are operating in that authority, those to whom they are ministering should submit to their authority and give them respect, honor, and support, regardless of whether the Minister is a man or woman.

A confusion of roles in marriage is generally the cause of divorce. The word divorce is really two words. The prefix "di" means two, and the base word "vorce" means force. Thus, divorce means two forces, instead of just one force in communal unity, are operating in the marriage; so, the disunity destroys the oneness of marriage.

The husband's headship responsibility is of divine ordering, as the husband is to protect, honor, support, and love his wife and family; and the duty of the husband is to lay down his life as Christ laid down His life for the Ekklesia. If a woman does not see that a man she is considering for marriage has these God-required Kingdom qualities, then she should not marry him. Likewise, if a man does not see that a woman he is considering for marriage will not appreciate his sacrificial support and loving protection under Christ, then he should not marry her.

Submission by the wife means promotion and honor, not subjugation and degradation. If a wife acts as if she still is single after marriage, then she is not properly under God's authority. If a woman cannot submit to her husband in his area authority, how can she be submitting to Christ who is her spiritual Bridegroom. If a husband cannot submit to his wife in her area of authority, how can he be submitted to Christ who is his bridegroom. Both the husband and wife are the bride of Christ.

Sometimes, a wife's refusal properly to follow God's redemptive Kingdom order is because of physical or emotional abuse, either by her husband or by what has happened in her past relationships. God understands that and wants to heal the wife. This is a major problem area that needs education, sometimes third-party counseling, or prayerful deliverance. More than anything else, though, the wounded wife needs to experience true, sacrificial love from her husband; and she can also look to Christ Jesus Who can give her true agape love through the Holy Spirit.

On the other hand, men, too, have been abused. Lots of men and some women have come back from actual war, fighting an enemy of the country with Post Traumatic Stress Disorder (PTSD). This can be a serious problem that may interfere with a spouse's sense of peace when the other spouse is having nightmares and sees and feels the enemy present. If a veteran spouse comes home and sees the toys all over the front yard or sees all the toys cluttering the house, the veteran spouse may suffer from PTSD because in the military, a soldier must be ready to fight 24 hours a day. He must keep weapons of warfare and protective helmets and the like always available at a moment's notice in the event of an attack on the military base or out in the war zone.

To end His model prayer, Jesus said in Matthew 6:14-15, "For if ye forgive men their trespasses, your heavenly Father will also forgive you: (15) But if ye forgive not men their trespasses, neither will your Father forgive your trespasses." Healing of the immortal female functioning soul starts with coming to the resolve that the man or prior husband or a woman or prior wife did not have any right from God to hurt or commit trespass of your sovereign royalty as the man or husband or the woman or wife as you were created by God as His royal child. The man or husband who hurts the woman or wife or the woman or wife who hurts the man or husband was a creature who also needed redemption by Christ Jesus. Yet, God's love (John 3:16) and Jesus' love (John 15:9) are eternal. Father God forgives, and Jesus forgives sins, and this is the pattern. The more a man or woman becomes Christ like, the more forgiving of others of their trespasses against them becomes a lifestyle.

Husband and father: Now, I will further analyze the biblical responsibility of the husband and father. The husband and father are personally responsible under the authority of Christ to be the marital and familial supportive, loving, and instructive benefactor of the wife and children in God's redemptive Kingdom order. The husband and father are always a servant like Christ who lays down His life for wife, family, and others in the community of Believers which he belongs (Mark 10:45). The husband and father's spiritual responsibility, as the protective and supportive equal, king, lord, and priest like the wife and mother of the home, also is to ensure the liberty through the Holy Spirit in spiritual matters to every member of the family. Yet, the wife is also an equal king, lord, and priest of the home, where she is the helpmeet to the husband and father, but with the same authority. Submission does not take away authority; it brings order and redemptive communication while exercising that authority.

Like his wife the husband, especially, must take to heart Galatians 2:20 and enter the crucifixion of Christ and allow Christ to live through him to minister to his wife and children. In that way Christ Jesus' pure agape love is transferred to his wife and children. However, like her husband, the wife has a responsibility to work out her own salvation (or transformation) of her soul with fear and trembling by allowing God to do His healing and transforming work in her (Philippians 2:12-13). Some men and women find it very difficult to submit to God and Christ Jesus because of past abuse from parents or a spouse or significant other. The lack of forgiveness of past relationships will cause problems in current relationships.

Jesus had authority as King here on earth but washed the feet of His disciples to show the importance of humility and servanthood (John 13: 13-16; Philippians 2:5-11). He was born a King of God's Kingdom (John 18:37). As has been said, both the husband and wife are kings, lords, and priests but more importantly are to be servants (Mark 10:44). Oftentimes, the father is a stricter disciplinarian than the mother.

For example, little Johnny is told by the father not to climb on the countertop in the Kitchen to obtain a cookie jar full of cookies. Little Johnny disobeys, climbs on the counter, reaches high to grab the cookie jar, and then falls with the cookie jar. The cookie jar breaks, and little Johnny cuts his hand, but the mother and father see he is okay but bleeding a little.

What is often the response by the mother and father? The mother runs to little Johnny, takes him to the sink, washes away the blood to see the cut, determines that it is not serious, gets bandages and antibacterial ointment, and medicates the wound, and kisses the wound to make the pain go away. The father says, "Johnny, I told you not to climb on the counter, and not to get the cookie jar without permission. Now, for your disobedience, you have extra chores to do. Additionally, you are to wipe off that blood on the floor, throw all the cookies into the trash because they might have glass in them; so, your mother does not have to do it. You see, Johnny, the reason your mother and I have rules is to protect you, so I hope you have learned to listen to us and obey us in the future." Little Johnny answers, "I am sorry, daddy." Then dad gives him a big hug.

The husband or father is especially required to be like Jesus in His relationship with the Ekklesia. The father or husband must lay down his life for his wife and family. If he is the only income earner, then he might have to work even if he is sick ,work overtime, or sometimes in a second job to support his family. If both the husband and wife are employed outside the home, then the husband must submit to the wife to help clean the house, help give the little children their baths, and help the children with their homework. When the wife and mother is sick, then the husband and father must cook the meals and clean house, do laundry, especially if the wife and/or mother is working a secular job or in her own business. That is just a small part of a husband and father laying down his own desires for the sake of his wife and children.

Ephesians 5:28-29 says, "So ought men (husbands) to love their wives as their own bodies. He that loveth his wife loveth himself. (29) For no man ever yet hated his own flesh; but nourisheth and cherisheth it, even as the Lord the church."

Submission to authority is a way of remaining humble before God. Ephesians 5: 21 says, "Submitting yourselves one to another in the fear of God." Thus, the husband and wife are to submit one to another for the betterment of the marriage and family.

There are times when the husband agrees to submit on a regular basis to the wife when it might involve her jurisdiction. We share costs of cleaning people who come every two weeks. I normally take care of watering, pruning, and fertilizing the flowers, plants, and lawn at our home. I also do my own laundry. I normally make breakfast for my wife and me, and I usually wash the dishes. My wife is much, much better at decorating the home. She is brilliant at it. That is her jurisdiction, and I ask her permission if I want to purchase something for the home. If she says that it is the wrong color or wrong style, I will not press the matter. I submit. I take out the trash, and often go and retrieve the mail. I often fill up the fuel tank in my wife's car. If my wife is sick, it is my pleasure to take care of her. By the way, she feels good about doing the same things for me. We take a mini vacation every ninety days. My wife shares with me our ministry, attends my podcasts, and helps me with pictures and covers for my books I publish, like her book.

Every single day, I pray for my family, law practice, ministry, health for friends who are sick and need financial help, and study my Bible. I write teachings and books from the illumination that the Holy Spirit imparts to me as He makes the word of God come alive to me. Yet, I still practice law as a profession. I am the one that normally knows when there is a demonic attack on the family, and I know how to resist the evil spirit; so, I do it as part of my protective duties (which Adam failed to do).

I am not saying men are better than women in praying against the kingdom of darkness. There are many great women prayer warriors, which I highly esteem and honor; and I call upon them occasionally to lift me up in prayer and to lift others who call me for prayer. I pray for my wife daily. I have a grandchild with severe food allergies, so I pray every day for his health; and I pray for a doctor to find a cure and for his protection. I pray for all my children and their spouses if they are married, my grandchildren, and my sister and cousins, and friends. I pray for my legal clients and special friends whom I led to the Lord.

Thus, the husband or father is primarily responsible, with his wife as his complementary helper, to pray against any demonic spirits or sins of the flesh from touching any member of the family or the greater household of faith.

I believe the husband or father is primarily responsible for discipline to maintain order in the home and family. Clear rules of behavior must be communicated to children, along with loving disciplinary actions when those rules are broken. The wife and mother and the husband and father must agree together concerning those rules of discipline. Discipline can never be abusive. It is not good to be too strict while the children are growing up and learning right and wrong.

For example, when our children got older the best discipline we used with the children was "lines." Every bad behavior, such as hitting, arguing, not sharing toys, stealing, and hiding a sibling's toys, not listening to parents, or failing to do chores required the discipline of "lines". When they are small, you just have to say, "No!" As they get older in school and can read and write, then they can write out a scripture based truth, such as, "I shall not steal my brother's toys." Or, the children write a particular scripture on a tablet 50 to 100 times. Believe me when I say my children learned quickly, as it often took more than an hour away from their play time to write out Ephesians 4;28, "Let him that stole steal no more."

Teenagers are a different problem completely. You must tell them that everything they have and are using, their bedroom, their clothes, their phone, their laptop, etc. is owned by the parents, and you as parents have the right as owners to take these things away until the teenager becomes obedient and repents of her disrespect and starts honoring you as the parents and starts following the rules established by the parents. Teenager discipline and discipleship is too long of a topic, and it is not the primary topic in this book. If you have a teenager, I will pray for you because you need it.

The father or husband is primarily responsible for keeping peace in the home. Whenever discipline is relegated solely to the wife and mother, sometimes the children's relationship with God is affected. So it is better that the father shares in an active way the disciplinary authority.

The father and husband has the duty to encourage and lead the family to focus on spiritual matters as directed by the Holy Spirit. The husband and father should head up the home Bible studies and prayer in the home. When my children were young, I would lay my hands on their heads and say a quick prayer to send them off to school. Ekklesia life is not just for women and children, but for the whole family, and the father and mother jointly must agree what fellowship to attend and how often, along with how to celebrate Christmas and Resurrection Sunday.

Prayer at meals and Ekklesia attendance should never be optional, just like reading the Bible or praying is not optional activities. Children learn by continuous repetition. Also, being respectful to parents and other siblings in the home is an important requirement. Honoring each other must be a mandated mindset to be encouraged by the father and husband in support of the mother and wife and encouraged by the wife and mother in support of the father and husband. Recognizing the gifts and special qualities of each member of the family should be encouraged by the father and husband and mother and wife. Honoring the wife and mother especially in front of the children should be the standard in the Christian home. Honoring the husband and father especially in front of the children should be the standard in the Christian home.

The husband or father and wife or mother are both responsible to teach the children that Ekklesia life is public and private, in the home and work, in schools and entertainment centers, and that when you visit other people's homes do not forget your spiritual Christian training that you have been taught.

Teach the children that saying "no" is not only the right thing to say, but also shows the child's maturity to others her age. If the child goes to someone's home and sees the friend's parents are away, and the teenager there asks, "Do you want to drink some alcohol?" The immediate answer is, "No!" The next step should be your child walking to the front door leaving the house where teenagers are drinking alcohol. The same thing goes with offering to smoke Marijuana or any other drugs. Just because something is legal under the secular government that does not mean that it is lawful under God's commandments. Certainly, neither alcohol nor marijuana are legal for young people under 21.

Both the father and mother must teach the children by example that Ekklesia practices are not mere behavior but the presence of Jesus' divine nature as the Life, Himself. Similarly, both the father and mother must teach the children there is no racism in the Ekklesia community life. There is no male or female gender bashing. Everyone is of equal importance because we all have been created by God. Every adult in the Ekklesia community is royalty as they are kings, lords, and priests. So the little princes and princesses in the home are trained to have faith with responsibility as they are underrulers of Christ in the Kingdom of God in training.

Even though a wife or mother or husband or father is called of the Spirit to be an apostle, prophet, evangelist, pastor, or teacher, she and he still must follow the redemptive Kingdom order in the family as established by God. The wife's spiritual equality with her husband coexists with her marital and family subordination to fulfill the offices of spouse and mother, and the same rules govern the husband. It is mandated that both husband and wife receive joint honor. The husband is mandated to be the greatest servant in the family like Christ is to the Ekklesia. There is no conflict. God has made the relationship between husbands and wives, parents and children, to be foundational in His kingdom and Christ is pattern to follow. Philippians 2:5-8 says, "Let this mind be in you, which was also in Christ Jesus: who, being in the form of God, thought it not robbery to be equal with God: But made Himself of no reputation.....and being found in fashion as a man, He humbled Himself."

If the wife is operating in her spiritual Ephesians 4:11 office engiftments, then the husband must submit to the words of God that comes from her. If the wife, husband, or any other Minister abuses the authority of an Ephesians 4:11 office, the Lord through the Holy Spirit will deal with him or her, personally, concerning that abuse of spiritual authority. Spiritual authority to minister and to preach the gospel of the Kingdom and repentance and remission of sins is given to both men and women equally as they each have an immortal male functioning born again spirit and an immortal female functioning soul; and both are kings, lords, and priests under the authority of the Godhead.

The Kingdom of God is righteous, peace, and joy in the Holy Spirit (Romans 14:17), so cultural modesty dictates that every action in Ekklesia community must be done in a way that maintains social dignity, decency, and order. For example, if an Ekklesia practice allowing dancing before the Lord as part of the worship, most women know they cannot be on the spiritual dance team wearing a red, low-cut blouse, or mini skirt. This type of dress would not be socially modest and would appeal to the flesh and be a bad witness to non-Believers in society and potentially a lustful temptation for the young men in the Ekklesia community. Social indiscretions sometime become fleshly distractions in Ekklesia gathering and fellowship.

In the kingdom of God spiritual rank is not based upon the societal distinctions of social rank, profession, culture, race, age, or whether one is a man or woman in the body. Ekklesia authority is not recognized or built on the attributes of the flesh or based upon the secular world's stature. Although God has the attributes of male and female, God is spirit and thus is male in expression. The Holy Spirit's anointing is masculine in function. Believers must respect the anointing in and on the Minister, whether a man or woman, not based upon the outward differences of the flesh, or regarding race, social status, or gender.

On the other hand, Paul recognized that social dress norms were genenrally subject to social convention and customs to which Ekklesia members should adhere so as not to be offensive, especially to newcomers. Many social dress norms are based upon the social history or culture of the nation.

Society expects people in various professions to dress in particular ways. Catholic priests wear collars and robes; some pastors wear suits while others dress more casually; judges wear robes; men lawyers wear suits and women lawyers wear business jackets, blouses, and matching pant suits; doctors wear white coats; teachers dress with modest but professional attire, brides wear wedding gowns, grooms wear tuxedos, soldiers wear uniforms, etc.

Yet, prostitutes dress in a way to provoke attention and lust of the flesh. Paul did not want women to dress in a way to violate cultural norms in Ekklesia community to appeal to the lust of the flesh or lust of the eyes, as the new liberty in the Spirit did not pertain to things of the flesh, but things of the Spirit.

For example, liberty in Christianity did not mean people could go around naked, as there is modesty in the cover-up. Liberty in Christianity also does not mean men and women can stop having good manners. With the advent of women's liberation in the secular world, some men have felt that they no longer must open doors for women. I disagree. Women's recognition as co-Ministers does not give men an excuse to be inconsiderate or ill-mannered toward them. Just because a man sends, and a woman accepts, a bouquet of flowers does not mean she is consenting to be owned, left alone, abused, or treated like an object by the man.

In 1 Corinthians 11:5, Paul said, "But every woman (or wife) who prays or prophesies with her head uncovered dishonors her head, for that is one and the same as if her head were shaved." The Greek for the word, dishonors is kataischuno, which means disfigurement or a lack of grace or disgrace. The word dishonors denote a lack of social grace, not a demeaning of the woman, or better, wife, to a subservient position. The wife was not disqualified nor forbidden to prophesy or pray in the New Testament first century Ekklesia meetings, but her spiritual authority must be exercised with decency, order, and conforming to social dress codes and social norms of behavior. The same rules apply to the men.

In 1 Corinthians 11:6, Paul said, "For if a woman (or wife) is not covered, let her also be shorn. But if it is shameful for a woman to be shorn or shaved, let her be covered." The Greek for the word shameful is aischron, which means "a lack of decorum or indecorum." In this case, prostitutes from the heathen temples who were having illicit sex with the sailors visiting the Corinthian port wore their heads shaven; so, the sailors could identify who they were. Still, after these prostitutes received salvation, they showed up in the Ekklesia looking like prostitutes with their heads shaven because their hair had not grown out.

In this case, Paul said they should put on a veil to cover their old reputation of shame, so as not socially to offend others while their hair was growing out. In this social setting, Paul's instructions had nothing to do with women in general being inferior in the Ekklesia to men, or women being disqualified to minister because of gender. Paul just did not want distraction in the Ekklesia services. Paul wanted women and men to conduct the meetings with decency and order. Furthermore, Paul said the women who were new converts, but not former prostitutes, but wives, should also be veiled; so, people would not think they were prostitutes and require their heads shaven.

Conformance to social customs and cultures that do not affect spiritual matters should be followed, and Paul was proclaiming this principle, not some male chauvinistic superiority. Every culture is different, and these cultural differences should be part of the social norms in the Ekklesia. Otherwise, the failure to follow the social norms in a particular culture can be a disruptive distraction to other members of the congregation during the meetings and may hinder Ekklesia growth.

In conclusion, Paul simply was saying that the social sentiments regarding dress code should be followed to avoid the hindrance of preaching and accepting of the gospel of the Kingdom and repentance and remission of sins.

During the first century Ekklesia, in the Greek and Asian cultures, for a wife to discard her veil was to renounce her modesty, and more importantly, was to renounce her honorable position with her husband.

The gospel message should never facilitate the destruction of, or cause disharmony in, the family unit, although interactions in the family must be adjusted through pastoral counseling to conform to the principles of the Bible to ensure and encourage each Believer has a personal relationship with the Lord and has loving fellowship with other Believers in the same Ekklesia community.

Unfortunately, many so-called biblical scholars have written their denominational doctrines misapplying these Scripture passages and others to try to sanctify or spiritualize their biases and prejudices against women in general.

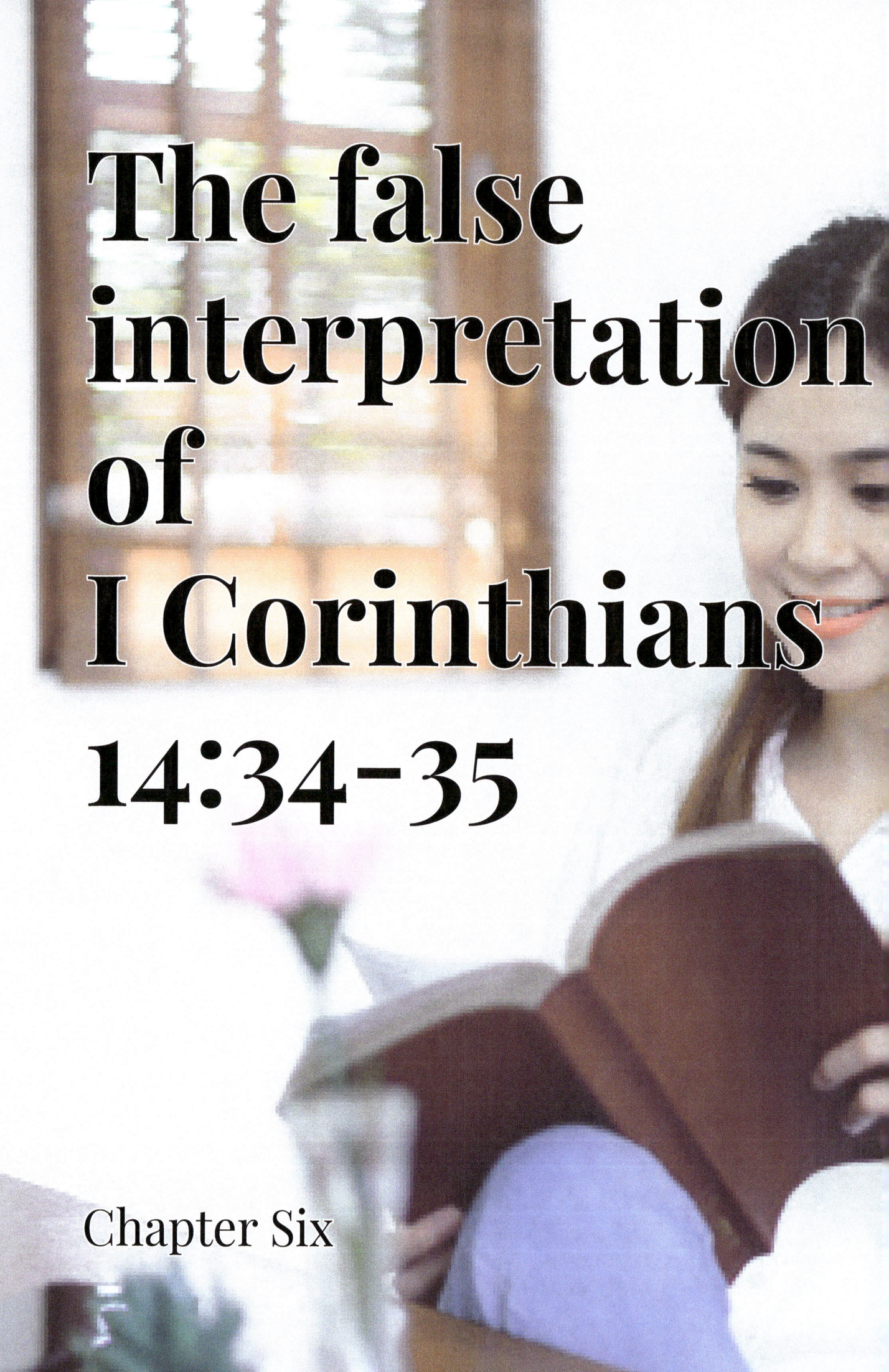

The false interpretation of I Corinthians 14:34-35

Chapter Six

CHAPTER SIX

The False Interpretation of 1 Corinthians 14:34-35

1 Corinthians 14:34-35 declares, "Let your women keep silent in the Ekklesia, for they are not permitted to speak; but they are to be submissive as the Law also says. And if they want to learn something, let them ask their own husbands at home; for it is shameful for women to speak in church."

At first glance, it seems that the scripture passage prohibits women in general from speaking in the Ekklesia meetings. However, 1 Corinthians 14:34-35 is inconsistent with Paul's sanctioning of women to publicly pray and prophesy in the Ekklesia meetings in the same discourse in 1 Corinthians 11:4-6. How can these two Scripture passages in the same book be harmonized since there should be no inconsistencies in God's inerrant word?

First, the Greek for women in these verses is really written in the singular instead of the plural as the Greek word gune is used, which designates a singular woman. Also, it should read as translated "Let the wives keep silent in the Ekklesia..." The word women or woman in these Scriptures should have been translated as wives or wife as, again, the same Greek word gune is used for both a woman and wife.

Similarly, the Greek for man or husband is the same Greek word, which is aner. Moreover, the proscription here really concerns a wife (gune) with her husband (aner) and cannot be a proscription against women in general and a man in general. Additionally, Paul said, "But they (wives) are to be submissive as the law also says."

First, the law referred to wives being submissive to husbands and did not require women in general to be submissive to men in general. Also, as was stated in a previous chapter, both men and women were submissive to each other. Women were not to talk to men who were not their husbands; so, submission to an unmarried or non-family member of the Ekklesia community was not part of the law. Also, a daughter was to be submissive to her father, but a son had the same obligation to be submissive to his father. The Greek word for submissive is hupotasso, which means to "subordinate oneself willingly to another in an orderly manner with honor, especially as between a husband and wife to each other."

The false translating Ekklesia leaders who want to disqualify women from ministry ignored that Paul was giving his instructions to wives and their husbands because the Scripture commands, ". . . let them ask their own husbands at home." The word them refers to the word the translators wrote down as women; so, the reference obviously is to married women not single women.

The reference in this scripture passage to aner and gune is to husbands and wives, as the translators were forced to write the English word husbands and wives later because they knew Paul would never tell a woman to submit and go home and live with a man not her husband.

Notwithstanding, the translators used the word women to spread a societal prejudice against women from being Ministers in their cultures at the probable objection of the women.

In modern times, a similar objection by women in the United States was protested in the 1970's to stop the tradition of a Minister concluding wedding ceremonies with "Now, I pronounce you man and wife." Many women took this statement to mean that the groom needed not be a husband but just a man, whereas the bride had to promise to be a wife as a sign of submission at the expense of being a woman.

 A close examination of the Greek word for "speak" in 1 Corinthians 14:34 will reveal further truth. The true translation is in Paul's use of the Greek verb, laleo. There are two Greek words for the English verbs speak or speaking. These Greek words are laleo and lego. Lego refers to the substance or intellectual part of a speech or message, which pertains to a well thought out statement, such as a teaching or sermon. However, leleo is just the reference to the sound itself, that comes out of the mouth. In fact, laleo is used also to refer to the sounds that come from animals and little babies that do not know a language, and it means an extended or random harangue.

Accordingly, laleo in this context refers to the sounds made by the jabbering of babies or infants before they learn how to speak the words of a particular language. Lalco comes from thc Grcck root word, lal and indicates, as pertaining to humans, the first words of a child in trying to talk, such as la, la, la or da, da, da.

Likewise, Paul used in this verse the present infinitive, lalein. This Greek infinitive tense word, lalein signifies ongoing or continuous babbling or talking amongst the Ekklesia wives while teaching, prophesying, or preaching, etc. was being vocalized by the Minister or Minsters. The whole purpose of 1 Corinthians, chapter 14 was to bring apostolic order in the Corinthian Ekklesia meetings. Consequently, these verses regarding wives must be interpreted in line with the Greek word used, the culture, scriptural context, and Paul's purpose of the whole chapter in addressing a particular problem of noise in the meetings.

In line with this reasoning, the Scripture should read, "Let your wives keep silent in the church, for they are not permitted to. . . (engage in la-la-la-ing or babbling or gossiping during the service)."

This point of view for translation purposes is seen by the Greek word Paul used for the word silent, which is segao from the root word sige. This Greek word means to hold peace, to hush, or better, to keep the noise down. It was not a word forbidding women to teach, to prophesy, to use the other verbal gifts, or to publicly proclaim the gospel of the Kingdom or message of repentance for remission of sins.

It is incorrect for Ekklesia leaders to use this passage of Scripture as biblical authority to conclude that women in general are not permitted to be Ephesians 4:11 Ministers or to forbid them to teach or speak in the Ekklesia meetings. Paul wanted all Believers to become spiritually mature, so he admonished the women to sit and listen to the preaching and teaching instead of talking about other things or visiting with women friends, or asking the husband to tell her immediately what the teacher or preacher means by his or her statements. This false teaching and practice of misapplying or mistranslating Greek to promote or foster a gender exclusion from ministry are based on ignorance and societal prejudice against women in general and is of the flesh and not of the Spirit and was not what Paul meant.

I made it clear that both men and women have immortal male functioning born again spirits and immortal female functioning souls, and that both men and women are the Bride of Christ.

Obviously, the injunction against wives to remain silent during the service was issued because the Corinthian wives, who were not generally educated (as education in the Greek culture was the privilege only of the men), often were asking questions of their husbands about what was being said by the Minister and disturbing the Ekklesia service with an ongoing harangue. The continuous chattering created an undertone of noise much like continuous babbling, and other Believers could not concentrate on what was being taught or preached.

Again, the whole chapter of 1 Corinthians 14 was written by Paul to put the Ekklesia services in cultural order. Apostles bring order! Paul also taught in this chapter on the proper public expression of tongues and prophecy, but not the denial of their use. Oftentimes, the same people who are against women being Ephesians 4:11 public Ministers are also against public Holy Spirit ministry gifts of tongues, interpretation of tongues, words of knowledge, words of wisdom, or words of prophecy.

Another important point is that Paul did not say the wives were never to speak or ask questions, as in verse 35 Paul tells the wives to ask these questions at home from their educated husbands who understood the gospel message and not disturb the meeting by asking questions during the Ekklesia service. He wanted them to learn and speak and ask questions; he just did not desire those questions to be asked in the open Ekklesia service where it was creating a disturbance.

In western cultures, there is the discipline of routine and respectful decorum, which is almost second nature or at least traditional. On the other hand, the meetings in religious circles of the time in the Eastern and Middle Eastern cultures, even in the heathen temples, engendered responsive impulsive, and emotional outbursts, which were not uncommon. The heathen temples were full of commotion, with little semblance of orderliness to which our Western cultures are accustomed in the Ekklesia meetings.

The quiet orderliness was not in the Jewish synagogues as well. People would suddenly stand up and start praying aloud or making a proclamation as in the parable offered by Jesus in contrasting the loud Pharisee with the quiet publican beating his chest standing in the rear of the synagogue (Luke 18:10-14). The custom was that a person who desired to read would rise in the synagogue, and the ruler of the synagogue would hand him a roll; and after reading, he might expound on the passage.

For example, in Luke 4:16-30, Jesus stood up and read from Isaiah 61:1-2. Likewise, if a visitor came, the ruler often would allow him to address the congregation as new insights or teachings were transmitted from synagogue to synagogue that way. There was much freedom to enter and leave the service as the summer heat would cause restlessness. Often, the emotional temperament set by local prejudice would incite a crowd to almost riot. If the speaker or teacher did or spoke something with which they disagreed, they would shout him down, and on occasion even try to assassinate the teacher as they tried to do to Jesus (Luke 4:28-29). In Acts 13:45, for example, the leaders offensively and violently interrupted Paul while speaking. Similarly, Acts 19: 21-41 reports of a violent Ekklesia scene in Ephesus. Ekklesia meetings were a much more animated place to attend in those days and culture.

There is no contradiction between 1 Corinthians Chapters 11 and 14, as Paul was merely being an Apostle who was bringing order to the Ekklesia meetings. 1 Corinthians 14:27 is revealing of Paul's intention when Paul said that people were to speak, "each in turn." Paul encouraged people not to interrupt each other (verses 29-30), which interruption was bringing disorder.

In fact, Paul told the prophets who were not speaking to "let the first keep silent" (verse 30). No one has ever interpreted this enjoinder of silence concerning prophets to mean the first prophet could never prophesy again publicly in the Ekklesia services. To keep order, if there was no interpretation of a tongue; then, Paul said let the one speaking in a tongue to remain silent (verse 28). Again, Paul's use of the word silent in 1 Corinthians 14: 28 cannot be interpreted to ban the speaking of tongues in the Ekklesia services, but only to state the rules for their use. Some denominations today have wrongfully gone as far as interpreting these passages, along with 1 Corinthians 13: 8-10, to say that verbal gifts, such as prophecy and tongues, are not for the Ekklesia today since the Ekklesia has the Canonized Word as the written voice of God for the New Testament Ekklesia. However, Paul was simply reasoning that prophecy was preferred over tongues because prophecy was in a known tongue and thus people could understand what was being said (1 Corinthians 14:4, 18-19). In fact, Paul makes it clear that all gifts must be exercised in a way to edify the Ekklesia in an orderly manner.

 Most Charismatics and Pentecostals believe that this preference does not prohibit the public speaking of tongues (1 Corinthians 14:26). The problem was that when unbelievers are present, an interpretation of the tongues should follow; so, that all those hearing could understand. On the day of Pentecost, those in the upper room speaking in tongues were heard by the crowd, and it was a witness to unbelievers that something supernatural was happening (Acts 2:6-8). Tongues are a sign to unbelievers (1 Corinthians 14:22). Other witnesses outside the upper room just thought the people were drunk. Notwithstanding, Paul was not against the public speaking of tongues, only that it be done with some guidelines to bring order in the Ekklesia services.

In fact, Paul said, "I thank God, I speak in tongues more than you all" (1 Corinthians 14:18). Therefore, why have some Ekklesia leaders interpreted the word "silent" in 1 Corinthians 14:34 to ban women from speaking in Ekklesia meetings when that same word used in the same chapter regarding the verbal gifts were not so interpreted? Ekklesia leaders cannot have it both ways! Paul just encouraged everything to be done for edification of the Body of Christ, "For God is not the author of confusion but of peace as in all the church of the saints" (1 Corinthians 14:33). Paul concludes in 1 Corinthians 14:40, "Let all things be done decently and in order." Therefore, the context of Paul's exhortation was not to exclude women from ministry, but merely to stop the noisy chattering, the speaking out of turn, and the doing of practices that were less edifying or interruptive to the Body of Christ.

Correspondingly, in 1 Corinthians 14:35, the Greek for the English word "shameful" is aischron, which means "a lack of decorum or indecorum." This Greek word is the same word used by Paul in 1 Corinthians 11:6, which says, "For if the woman be not covered, let her also be shorn: but if it be a shame for a woman to be shorn or shaven, let her be covered." It is a word meaning out of order or disorderly. Again, Paul wanted to bring order and decorum to the services that were not traditionally or culturally present as Believers now practice in the Western world. His purpose was not to put shame on women or disallowing them to minister in public, but to stop the shameful and undignified rowdy commotion caused by some of the wives in conversing with their husbands or others wives during the service.

When the woman, like the man, was redeemed, shame was taken away (Romans 8:1), and both man and woman were naked but without shame in the original creation design (Genesis 2: 25). Shame came after sin was committed. Once sin is taken away through the precious spilt blood of Jesus, the shame is also removed for both men and women, not just for the men alone. So, if shame has been taken away, then why shame the women by saying they are not qualified to be a king, lord, priest, ambassador, and soldier of God in His Kingdom?

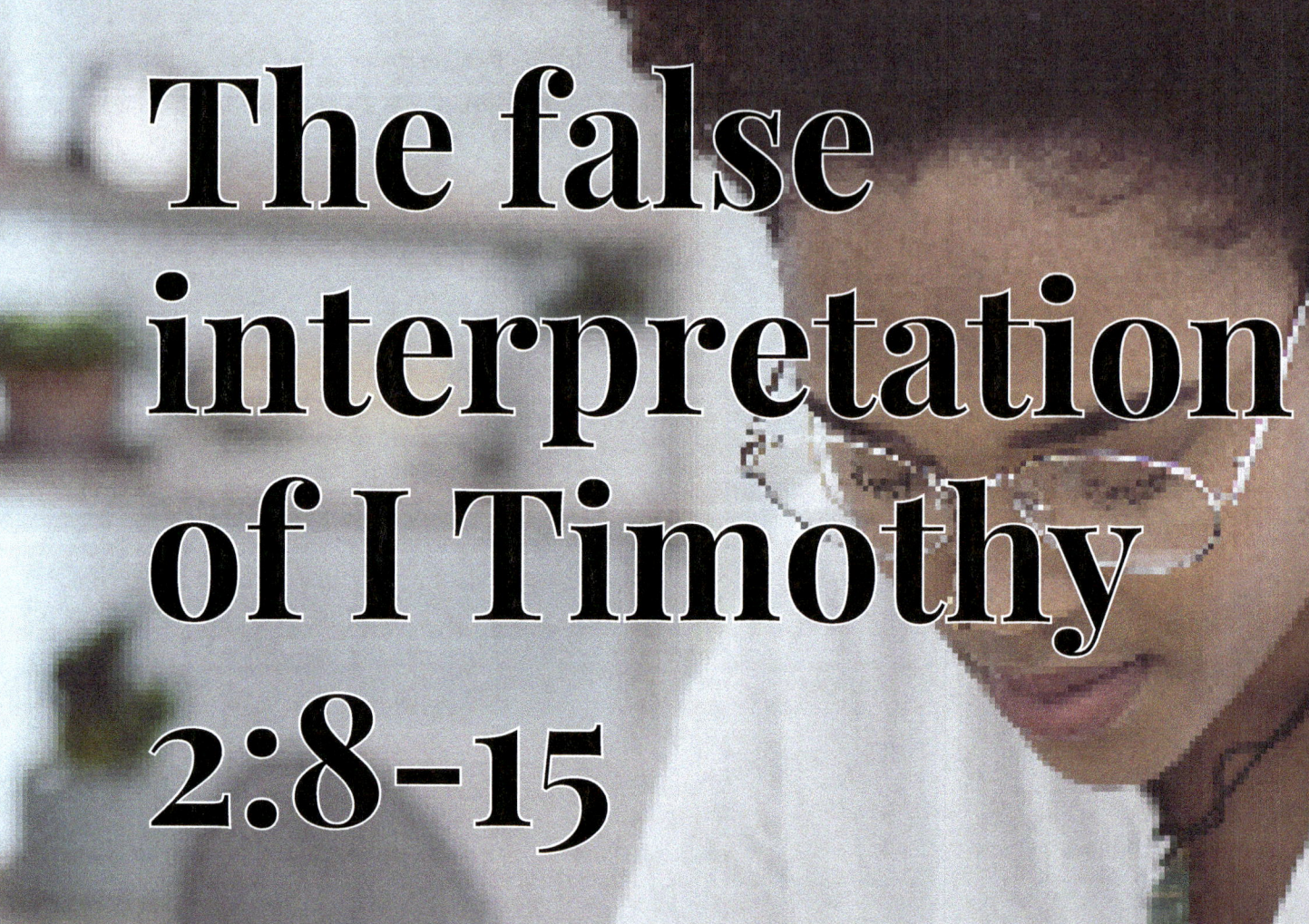

The false interpretation of I Timothy 2:8-15

Chapter Seven

CHAPTER SEVEN

The False Interpretation of 1 Timothy 2:8-15

In 1 Timothy 2: 8-15 this controversial subject continues: "I will therefore that men pray everywhere, lifting up holy hands, without wrath and doubting. (9) In like manner also, that women adorn themselves in modest apparel, with shamefacedness and sobriety; not with braided hair, or gold, or pearls, or costly array; (10) But (which becometh women professing godliness) with good works. (11) Let the woman learn in silence with all subjection. (12) But I suffer not a woman to teach, nor to usurp authority over the man, but to be in silence. (13) For Adam was first formed, then Eve. (14) And Adam was not deceived, but the woman being deceived was in the transgression. (15) Notwithstanding she shall be saved in childbearing, if they continue in faith and charity and holiness with sobriety."

To begin with, in verse 8 Paul is again addressing the issue of order in the Ekklesia, as some men had been displaying wrath and doubting among themselves in prayer meetings. Therefore, they were contradicting the admonition of lifting holy hands when they were praying.

Paul begins his exhortation to the women with the phrase, "In like manner also, that women...." The phrase, "In like manner also ..." means that Paul is drawing a parallel to discuss about the women the same subject of praying improperly as he just had done with the men. Women are to be praying while only adorning themselves with modest apparel, with propriety and moderation. Again, the Apostle is instructing the Ekklesia to do things in decency and order during Ekklesia prayer services. His instruction is not a prohibition to stop women from publicly praying, teaching, preaching, prophesying, or any other public ministry.

How many times have we seen people dress up to be noticed in an Ekklesia meeting? Paul did not want prayer time in church to become a fashion show for the women, nor to become a flesh-out show for the men where wrath and doubting were expressed.

Anger amongst the men is a real problem, especially in certain cultures, where some are easily offended. Without faith it is impossible to please God (Hebrews 11:6), and doubt comes from the meaning of being double minded. Thus, the men were being double minded, not believing that their prayers would be answered. As with those wives whom Paul said should remain veiled when they prayed and prophesied in 1 Corinthians 11:5, Paul instructed the women to wear modest apparel and assemble in a temperate, acceptable, and conservative manner when they were praying. Paul wanted to ensure that the attention was to be drawn to God, not to the Believers in the way they were dressed and their actions.

In the Gentile cultures, the women customarily would braid gold coins or expensive pearls or jewels in their hair and would wear costly clothing. Wives were permitted in marriage to own what they wore in clothing and jewelry. In the event of divorce, the wives were only allowed to take with them whatever apparel and jewelry woven into their hair they had on at the time. Hence, especially in the Middle East, Gentile women started acquiring wealth in the form of jewelry, coins, precious stones, and anything they could wear that had intrinsic value. Even today, it is interesting that wives in most cultures are more apt to desire jewelry as gifts at Christmas, Mother's Day, anniversaries, birthdays, Valentine's Day, etc. in the United States and Europe. "Diamonds are a girl's best friend" were the lyrics of a popular song in the 50's. Historically, women from India, Pakistan, the Middle East, and the Far East collect jewelry as a status symbol. Watch how some women will gather around another woman who walks into a room with a big engagement or wedding ring which has a large diamond ("rock") as its setting. When you encounter these wives and women, think about the historical, cultural reasons why value was placed on jewelry.

1 Timothy 2: 11-15 really do not address the public exercise of teaching by women, but rather the private, domestic life between a husband and wife. Paul changes his thought from public to private because he went from men and women in verses 8 through 10 to the singular wife and singular husband in verses 11 through 15. Likewise, Paul excluded the article before the word woman in the Greek, even though in the translation in English sometimes is included.

If Paul had said the woman, it perhaps could be argued that the reference was to a teaching for the universal woman as a gender as opposed to the instruction for a wife in intimate relationship with her husband. If Paul had been continuing the teaching of verses 8 and 9 in verses 11 through 15, verse 11 would have said in the Greek "Let the woman learn in silence with all subjection." The Greek for the word subjection is hupotage, from the Greek word hupotasso, which is a voluntary submission of the wife to her husband in exchange for the husband honoring his wife as part of the marriage covenant. The husband's covenant is to lay down his life daily as a servant provider for and spiritual joint leader with the wife and children for their wellbeing. Subjection is not to be interpreted as placing a wife in a lower level. She is still a king, lord, priest, ambassador, soldier, and betrothed in God's Kingdom.

Yet, women were never to submit intimately to anyone but their husbands in the Greek culture and in the Jewish culture, and the culture must be read into the context of this Scripture passage for proper understanding. Hence, Paul had to be referring to a wife instead of a woman. Similarly, in 1 Timothy 2:15, Paul uses the singular female personal pronoun, she, as the subject of the sentence, not the plural pronoun, they, when he says, "Notwithstanding she shall be saved in childbearing, if they (she) continue in faith and charity and holiness with sobriety." The word "they" in the Scripture cannot refer to the singular subject "she" in the same sentence. The word must refer to a husband and wife. Paul is saying if the husband and wife continue to practice intimate fidelity.

This exhortation by Paul is that a wife is not to teach or force her opinions on her husband, as this practice may cause some husbands to reject the gospel of the Kingdom of God; and they may not repent for the remission of sins nor accept Jesus Christ as Lord and Savior. Since the prohibition not to teach refers not to women in general but to a wife in relationship with her husband, it cannot be a supportive Scripture forbidding women from publicly teaching or preaching the Gospel.

In 1 Peter 3:1-4, Peter speaks to the wives to bring voluntary humility but not enslavement: "Likewise, ye wives, be in subjection to your own husbands; that, if any obey not the word, they also may without the word be won by the conversation of the wives; (2) While they behold your chaste conversation coupled with fear. (3) Whose adorning let it not be that outward adorning of plaiting the hair, and of wearing of gold, or of putting on of apparel; (4) But let it be the hidden man (immortal male functioning born again spirit) of the heart, in that which is not corruptible, even the ornament of a meek and quiet spirit, which is in the sight of God of great price." Peter gives similar instructions to the Ekklesia about the same problem, but his Holy Spirit inspired words clearly address husbands and wives in the redemptive Kingdom order of the Ekklesia family.

Again, the word submissive in 1 Peter 3:1 is the Greek word, hupotasso, a derivative word as in 1 Timothy 2:11 hupotage, which means for a wife to subordinate herself willingly to her husband in an orderly manner in exchange for honor as an equal king, lord, priest, ambassador, and soldier in the Kingdom of God. Peter makes it clear that submission by the wife is in exchange for honor from the husband.

In fact, the wife's submission in 1 Peter 3:1 is conditioned upon her receiving the honor referred to in 1 Peter 3:7, where Peter brings correction to the husbands as well: "Husbands, likewise, dwell with them (wife) with understanding, giving honor to the wife, as to the weaker vessel, and as being heirs together of the grace of life, that your prayers may not be hindered."

Giving honor to someone is holding them in high esteem, paying them tribute and support. The Greek word for honor is the word, time (pronounced "tee-may") which means "to esteem in the highest degree to the position of paying tribute money to them as a dignitary, whose presence is to be considered precious, spiritually beneficial and costly."

It bears repeating that the family unit is patterned after the Godhead, which consists of God the Father, God the Word and Jesus' humanity nature as the Son of God, and God the Holy Spirit, who are equal but in the redemptive plan have a Kingdom order of orderly and honorable humility. Similarly, the wife and husband are equals as joint heirs in Christ. If the husband does not treat his wife with honor, then his prayers will be hindered. These Scriptures give an extraordinarily strong warning and incentive for husbands to honor their wives. Most husbands would not want God to turn His ear away from their prayers of petition, thanksgiving, or supplication.

Here is what is supposed to happen when the wife properly submits to her spiritual husband in God's redemptive plan and Kingdom order. As Christ Jesus submitted to the Father, the Father highly exalted or highly esteemed Him, giving Him the name above every other name, that at the very mention of His name, every knee should bow in honor and every tongue shall confess that He is Lord to the glory of the Father (Philippians 2:8-11). Those who humble themselves before God in His redemptive Kingdom order, God will exalt. James 4:6,10 proclaims God's motive and intent: "God resists the proud, but gives grace to the humble. . . Humble yourselves in the sight of the Lord, and He will lift you up." There is no Biblical dishonor in submission. To the contrary, there is Biblical honor only after Biblical submission.

These Scriptures cannot be used to subjugate women into mere chattel, or to be dishonored as being denied equality of the graces, crowns, ministries, or gifts of God. In the Kingdom of God, voluntary submission to God results in honor. Jesus said in Mark 10:42-43, "... Ye know that they which are accounted to rule over the Gentiles exercise lordship over them; and their great one's exercise authority upon them. (43) But so shall it not be among you: but whosoever will be great among you, shall be your (servant) minister."

Traditionally, when a husband and wife are married, the husband gives the wife his family name to honor her, not to subject her to his every whim. Honor is given to the wife because she has humbled herself in God's divine order, just as Christ humbled Himself to His Father and was highly honored (Philippians 2:5-11). The wife is the recipient of honor from her husband as she adjusts her single life into a married life with her husband in the divine order of God's redemptive Kingdom order and plan in exchange for her honor from the husband.

One of the greatest examples of this submission with honor principle is in Ephesians 5:22-33. The context of the passage is revealed in verse 21, which says, "Submitting to one another in the fear of God." Submission to each other is a way of life for Believers, husband and wife, although it has become a red flag word because some husbands degraded and demoted their wives and each other for centuries. In Ephesians 5:22, wives are taught to submit to their husbands as unto the Lord Jesus Christ just like Christ Jesus submitted to Father God. A wife is to accept her husband's spiritual leadership in the marriage, so long as the husband becomes

Christ-like in his character and actions as the spiritual headship of the home who lays down his life in preference and honor to his wife and caring for his children and as the one seeking continuous spiritual leadership in the home with the gifts of the Spirit with agape love.

However, adjustments into a married life by the wife cannot be forced by the husband, but must be given freely by the wife based upon her loving trust in her husband's spiritual leadership in expectation of being honored. Therefore, this Scripture passage is a reference to God's redemptive Kingdom order and plan where the husband and wife are equals in authority and mission. The pattern is the same when a member of the Godhead decides who has the lead here on earth. God the Father was the husband of Israel in the wilderness (Isaiah 54:5). God the Word with Jesus' humanity nature had authority on earth when Christ Jesus came to earth (John 17:2-3). After Jesus ascended, the Holy Spirit came with authority (John 16:13). Every member of the Godhead intently had authority here on earth. He submitted himself to the other members of the Godhead.

Ephesians 5:23 maintains that husbands are marital spiritual heads of their wives the same way Christ is the spiritual Head of the Ekklesia, as He is the Savior, Lord, Intercessor, and Head of His body. Christ identified with the Betrothed that was full of sin, but He substituted Himself to suffer and die a cruel death on a Roman Cross for her benefit, not enslavement and infernal damnation. Christ became sin for unbelievers, as Christ knew no sin; yet die for sinners who believe so that Believers may be the righteousness of God in Christ (2 Corinthians 5:21).

Christ's relationship with the Ekklesia is the pattern regarding the responsibility of the husband toward the voluntary submissive wife, which is one of substitutionary sacrifices for the wife's benefit. In line with Christ's pattern, the submission in Ephesians 5:22 was balanced and conditioned upon the sacrificial love in Ephesians 5:25, which says, "Husbands, love your wives, even as Christ also loved the church, and gave Himself for it." Christ laid down His life for His Betrothed, and husbands are exhorted that this is the pattern as to how a husband is to honor his wife and lay down his life for her.

Men should start this practice of honoring their wives even before they marry as Christ presented the example, as He died for His Betrothed while His Betrothed was yet a sinner (Romans 5:8) and before She, as His Betrothed, qualified to be a Bride in all her glory (Ephesians 5:27).

Ephesians 5:28 asserts, "So husbands ought to love their wives as their own bodies. He that loveth his wife loveth himself." Being the one with spiritual headship means that husbands are not to "flesh out" when dealing with their wives and children but are exhorted to be an example in the home in maintaining their bodies as the Temple of the Lord. This means the husband is to be the leader in the home in nurturing the wife and family with the fruit of the Spirit instead of the works of the flesh (Galatians 5:19-23).

Adam's work assignment preceded marriage in the Garden of Eden. In like fashion, men should get a job, business, or investment income stream prior to getting married; so, husbands can pay proper tribute or support to honor their wives. Paul concludes in Ephesians 5:33 that: "Nevertheless let every one of you in particular so love his wife even as himself; and the wife see that she reverences her husband." Honor by the husband returns respect by the wife. The principle is consistent in that love, help-mate, and honor are to be expressed together, which will result in respect in return. They go together like God the Father, God the Word, and God the Holy Spirit, who have total honor, respect, and love for each other.

Christ commanded His Betrothed (both men and women) to preach the gospel of the Kingdom (Matthew 24:14) and repentance and the remission of sins (Luke 24:47) everywhere (Acts 1:18). Ephesians 4:7,11-13 says, "But unto every one of us (men and women) is given grace according to the measure of the gift of Christ... (11) And He gave (to men and women) some, apostles; and some, prophets; and some, evangelists; and some, pastors and teachers; (12) For the perfecting of the saints (both men and women), for the work of the ministry (by both men and women), for the edifying of the body (both men and women) of Christ: (13) Till we all (men and women) come in the unity of the faith, and of the knowledge of the Son of God, unto a perfect man (both men and women having their immortal female functioning souls be spiritually transformed like the perfect, sinless, righteous, and holy immortal male functioning born again spirit), unto the measure of the stature of the fulness of Christ."

Consequently, Paul taught that the Body of Christ consists of both men and women as equal Ministers, as equal Believers. Both men and women are continuously developing and transforming their immortal female functioning souls to become the righteous and holy Betrothed of Christ Jesus. Again, there is no distinction between male and female in God's spiritual Kingdom when it comes to ministry (Galatians 3:28).

Christ never commanded submission of His Betrothed by coercion or forcing the obedience of members of His Body and Ekklesia. No! Christ desires His Betrothed to serve Him willingly, with honor, with her whole immortal male functioning born again spirit and immortal female functioning soul, ready to pour out her life for Him because of His love for her was unto His death. This, too, is the pattern for husbands and eventually both men and women as unto the Lord.

The most important benefit of submission is the immortal female functioning soul sanctification and cleansing leading to glorification, perfection, righteousness, and holiness, which is bestowed honor in the eyes of God as the Ekklesia matures to the point of oneness in harmonious communion. Ephesians 5:27 gives the reward for submission by the Betrothed, "That He might present her to Himself a glorious Ekklesia, not having spot, or wrinkle, or any such thing; but that she should be holy and without blemish."

Adjusting her life to being married to her husband the wife can insist that the husband must be Christ-like. Submission is given by the wife in exchange for honor because the husband has promised in faithfulness and care that he in the redemptive Kingdom order will give up his personal life to maintain, fulfill, and complete his responsibilities to his wife and family in God's kingdom.

The pattern Christ gave for us is that the husband's sacrifice to support and esteem His Betrothed had to be proven prior to the wedding ceremony. The wife should show honor and respect to her husband in expectation of honor and respect from the husband in return. Perhaps the old traditional words requested or said by the bride in the wedding ceremony to "honor and obey" really should have been that the "bride promises to be a helpful and loving wife, so long as the husband honors her."

On the other hand, what we have seen amongst many of the men throughout history who have become leaders in the traditional denomination old religious orders are the interpretation of these various Scriptures discussed in this book in such a way as to make women have less honor, less authority, and less respect in the Ekklesia than the men. They have also used these Scriptures to justify their actions of subjugating the women to positions of second-class or third-class citizens in the Kingdom of God. Additionally, they have interpreted these scriptures to disqualify women from being Ephesians 4:11 Ministers.

This subjugation of women has hindered the growth of God's Kingdom and has grieved the Holy Spirit. The women have come to the Ekklesia for sanctuary and protection from ill treatment by their husbands in many cases who have followed the anti-women customs historically in the fallen secular world. God has heard their cries of injustice. Women Believers are anointed of God the same as men Believers. God does not give a less powerful anointing to women Believers just because they are women. It begs to be said over and over to sink in the truth that there is no distinction between male and female in God's kingdom regarding ministry (Galatians 3:28).

Husbands and men Believers, like it or not, wives and women Believers qualify as God's anointed Ministers the same as husbands and men Believers, whom God will protect; so, treat them with honor and respect. Likewise, wives and women Believers treat husbands and men Believers who equally are anointed and called as anointed Ministers; so, give them honor and respect. Honor and respect the calling and anointing on the Ephesian 4:11 Ministers, whether a man Believer or a woman Believer.

One of the greatest honors bestowed upon a woman was Mary of Bethany, a virtuous single woman, who submitted to Christ Jesus, as her spiritual Headship and Lord, and lovingly anointed His head, feet, and body with a costly fragrant perfumed oil. Jesus recognized her as a symbol of the Ekklesia pattern for the Betrothed of the Lord as she poured out the costly perfume, costing about a year's wages, on the head, feet, and body of Jesus just days before His crucifixion (Matthew 26:12). As Jesus was being beaten and then dying on the Roman Cross, the fragrant aroma of costly ointment was still on Him to remind Him of the love that one representing His Betrothed had for Him.

The revelation Jesus wanted everyone to see was that this virtuous woman, who showed extravagant love, is to be the pattern for the honor, love, respect of the Body of Christ in the final days to perfect His Betrothed to receive glorious honor. Her extreme love for the Lord was recognized in scripture by the Lord with eternal honor.

Matthew 26:7 -13 says, "There came unto him a woman having an alabaster box of very precious ointment, and poured it on his head, as He sat at meat. (8) But when His disciples saw it, they had indignation, saying, 'To what purpose is this waste? (9) For this ointment might have been sold for much and given to the poor. (10) When Jesus understood it, He said unto them, 'Why trouble ye the woman? For she hath wrought a good work upon Me. (11) For ye have the poor always with you; but Me ye have not always. (12) For in that she hath poured this ointment on My body, she did it for my burial.' (13) Verily I say unto you, 'Wheresoever this gospel shall be preached in the whole world, there shall also this, that this woman hath done, be told for a memorial of her.'"

This pattern for total, extreme love of the Lord as His Betrothed is required of the end time Believes before the Lord returns. Correspondingly, this kind of extravagant expenditure upon the body of Christ will cause criticism by the religious leaders looking on because it will appear to be a waste of money, approaching fanaticism. Moreover, this extreme love of Christ's body is required to bring forth Christ's glorious Bride without spot or wrinkle.

I thank God, today, that we still have women Believers desiring to pour out their alabaster flask of very costly fragrant ointment on the body of Christ. In return, they are told that their unselfish efforts are a waste of time and money. The women have a God-ordained tendency to express their total love of Jesus; so, that the body of Christ can experience the crucifixion of self to be sanctified and cleansed to become spiritually mature as Christ's glorious future wife.

The women Believers seem to be especially equipped to carry the body of Christ into the next great move of the Spirit for Betrothed extravagant love leading to glorification. The actions of love of the wife to the husband can show and lead the husband to conform his actions of love and humility towards becoming one of the sanctified, perfected multi-Believers Betrothed of Christ, just as each Believer was given a perfectly matured, holy, new, immortal male functioning born again spirit (1 Peter 1:23; Hebrews 12:23; Ephesians 4:24; Colossians 3:10).

Here Is another important point concerning 1 Timothy 2:11-15; Again, the Greek makes no distinction between the words man and husband or woman and wife. The Greek word in this Scripture for man and husband, again, is aner while the Greek word for woman and wife, again, is gune. Hence, the translators could have easily said, "Let a wife learn in silence with all submission, and I do not permit a wife to require submission of the husband as his teacher or to have dictatorial authority over her husband, but to be in silence."

The Greek word for submission means conditional submission only if the wife is being honored in her position as joint heirs of the kingdom blessings in Christ Jesus. In 1 Timothy 2:13-14 Paul's reference to the first husband and first wife, Adam, and Eve, also supports this interpretation. These verses concluding chapter 2 of 1 Timothy are merely a reference to a family matter between a husband and wife, not a prohibition against women in general from being apostles, prophets, evangelists, pastors, or teachers or having any other gifts in aiding her ministry call in the body of Christ.

Paul was bringing order to a local problem of some domineering wives who were too offensive in their behavior, and perhaps complaints were being registered of this self-righteous and sense of superiority conduct in public prayer meetings and in home life. These unruly wives were dishonoring themselves, their husbands, and the local Ekklesia by not being loving with humility, and with honor to their husbands; but were trying to lord over their husbands as ones having superior knowledge as teachers because they were more mature having been saved for a season while their husbands were newly saved and young Believers in Christ. Still, Paul does not say that the wives were dishonoring themselves by publicly teaching with God's wisdom, knowledge, and understanding to the population of men and women when they gathered as a whole Ekklesia, or in the traditional teaching duties of mothers and grandmothers in the homes, or as mature women teaching younger women how to be godly wives.

For example, forbidding a mother to teach her children would be in contradiction to other Scriptures. Similarly, in Titus 2:2-4, Paul instructed older mature women to be "teachers of good things-- that they admonish the young women to love their husbands, to love their children, to be discreet, chaste, homemakers, good, obedient to their own husbands, that the word of God may not be blasphemed." However, the wife was not to lay down the law or be overly domineering to her husband, because the husband may reject the gospel of the Kingdom and will not repent for the remission of sins if she did. Paul knew that husbands, especially, must come to the gospel of the Kingdom voluntarily, without coercion, as they may reject being force-fed by preaching or teaching from their wives. The church was young and Paul did not want division between husbands and wives.

On the other hand, husbands need to learn to honor the anointing of God on their wives, as the wives are joint heirs of God's Kingdom of righteousness, peace, and joy in the Holy Spirit. Additionally, wives need to respect the anointing of God on their husbands. The anointing is what destroys the yokes of bondage (Isaiah 10:27) of the curse and takes away the burden of sins in people's lives; so, the anointing is not designed to put people in unwanted coercive bondage nor strap them with undue burdens. The anointing brings liberty from illness and liberty against the abiding influence of demonic spirits and cultural prejudices.

For example, fathers and mothers willingly have entered a yoke to support and lovingly raise their children. However, this is a love yoke fulfilling the will of God. Bondage through coercion and voluntarily agreeing to the assumption of responsibility are two different ways of fulfilling scripture. The first is religion, whereas the second is freedom of choice.

A father and mother cannot say that their children are an unwanted yoke of bondage. Even secular society has laws demanding that fathers and mothers nourish and support their children during their minority, as they are weaker vessels. Children are to submit to their parents, and the parents are to support and render care to the welfare of their children. This, too, is the divine Kingdom order of God's redemptive plan. Everyone is to submit, honor, and respect each other as servants to others in the Kingdom of God here on earth as it is in heaven (Matthew 6:10; Ephesians 5:22). Jesus said whoever wants to be first is to be the servant of all (Mark 9:35).

The conclusion is plain that the husband is to treat his wife as Christ treats His Ekklesia, by laying down his life for his wife. Jesus stated the principle in John 12:25-26: "He (generic for both men and women) that loveth his life shall lose it; and he (both men and women) that hateth his life in this world shall keep it unto life eternal. (26) If any man (generic for both men and women) serves Me, let him follow Me; and where I am, there shall also My servant (both men and women) be: if any man (both men and women) serves Me, him (both men and women) will my Father honour."

Romans 13:7 commands, "Render therefore to all their dues: tribute to whom tribute is due; custom to whom custom; fear to whom fear; honour to whom honour." The principle involved is clear: spiritual honor and service to another returns honor in God's redemption Kingdom order and plan.

In 1 Timothy 2:12 Paul advises wives not to try to teach their husbands in a dictatorial, domineering, or vociferous manner, for this would tend to cause husbands to reject the gospel of the Kingdom, the authority in the Ekklesia, and God's redemptive plan and Kingdom order of both men and women. However, it would be improper to interpret this Scripture to forbid public ministry of teaching by women. Scriptures cannot be interpreted to mean that women are somehow to receive less honor than the men, or that wives should receive less honor than their husbands. Both men and women are the multi-members of the Bride of Christ, and Christ died a cruel death for His Bride to be; both men and women Believers.

As an illustration, Priscilla stood in the office of a teacher with her husband, Aquilla. Apollos needed correction in his doctrine; so, Acts 18:26 conveys what happened: "And he (Apollos) began to speak boldly in the synagogue: whom when Aquila and Priscilla had heard, they took him unto them (both Aquilla and Priscilla), and (both Aquilla and Priscilla) expounded unto him the way of God more perfectly." A more accurate translation of the Greek of that scripture would reference Priscilla before Aquilla, as Priscilla had the greater call as a teacher. In Romans 16:3, Paul purposefully and distinctly grants Priscilla the priority over Aquilla, "Greet Priscilla and Aquila my helpers in Christ Jesus." Paul also put Priscilla before Aquilla in Acts 8:18 and 2 Timothy 4:19. Paul was accepting Priscilla's greater calling on her life than her husband's and acknowledging Priscilla's teaching anointing with greater honor.

The word silence in 1 Timothy 2:11 is a wrong translation in the King James (probably a local prejudice) which was corrected in the American Standard Version as "in quietness." The Greek word used here is hesuchia, which means, "desisting from bustle or disturbing language or being quiet, tranquil, and at peace during appropriate times." This Greek word comes from the word hesuchios, which means "to keep one's seat in a sedentary way, to be still, to be undisturbing, to remain peaceable, or to sit in a quiet manner."

The same Greek word here was properly translated as quiet and quietness in the King James Version in 1 Thessalonians 4:11 and 2 Thessalonians 3:12. The Greek word really means tranquility, which denotes the absence of strife or disturbance or arguing type of speech. The prohibition does not forbid all speech, but only that type of speech that is bickering, nagging, or domineering, and does not address speech which is edifying, exhorting, comforting, or teaching to the body of Christ.

The refrain from this type of speech is the same prohibition which Paul used in 1 Corinthians 14:29-30, so as not to bring confusion in the exercise of tongues and prophecy. To make sure that his statements would be clearer, Paul said "You all may prophesy, one by one!" (1 Corinthians 14:31). The words "all may prophesy" was meant by Paul to include both men and women. Likewise, 1 Corinthians 11:4-5 makes it clear that men and women should publicly pray and prophesy in the New Testament Ekklesia, but Paul instructs the Believers that everything must be done in an orderly manner. The instruction of Paul was for greater civility and respect for the anointed servant Minister who was speaking without interruption or noise, and not the prohibition of women not to minister in Ekklesia or forbid women from exercising verbal gifts, especially in the Ekklesia fellowship meetings.

If there were an absolute silence of women in the Ekklesia as some historical old religious order leaders contend, like Luther interpreted these verses, then women would not be allowed to sing on the praise and worship team, or even sing in the congregation seats. In fact, some men in leadership in history have interpreted these verses to exclude women even from public worship. In the days of Johann Sebastian Bach, the German Lutheran old religious practice used 1 Timothy 2:11 to exclude women from singing hymns in the Ekklesia. Thus, the women probably called the Lutheran Ekklesia in that country in those days "The Church of the Tenors and Baritones."

Why did a Believer not stand up and declare the truth from Scripture? Were Believers that ignorant about the Greek Language? Were Believers in Europe that unknowledgeable about the Eastern and Middle Eastern Cultures? On the other hand, was this woman bashing just a male prejudice to maintain their pseudo male superiority in the European society and Ekklesia?

Even today, in France, Spain, Portugal, Germany, United Kingdom, United States, Mexico, South America, Africa, India, Russia, China and elsewhere, men are in basically control with the societal and ecclesiastical authority and power; and some denominational leaders have purposely interpreted these Scriptural passages out of context to enhance and maintain their positions as all male Pastors and leaders.

In the Kingdom of God both the man and woman are called to become doulos or love servants of Christ Jesus. A doulos in the Kingdom of God is a position of great honor, a very peculiar position indeed. In 1 Peter 2:9 God called men and women Believers together, "But ye are a chosen generation, a royal priesthood, a holy nation, a peculiar people; that ye should shew forth the praises of Him who hath called you out of darkness into His marvelous light."

The people who have obtained mercy through Christ Jesus are the same people God declared to be part of a "chosen generation, a royal priesthood, a holy nation, a peculiar people." Since men and women both have received the mercy of God unto salvation, then both men and women are called of God to be His royal kings, lords, priests, ambassadors, and soldiers. If God considers women to have the same royalty and priestly calling as men, then why would finite men disagree?

Kingly authority is given to both men and women to do priestly services to minister reconciliation as ambassadors of Christ (2 Corinthians 5:18, 20). The doulos was about the Master's business, not his or her own business. The peculiar servant, or doulos, was a unique person in society with much delegated authority and power from the Master; but there was nothing he or she could call his or her own. The peculiar people were true male and female Ambassadors of the Master (Jesus Christ) sent to do His Father's business from heaven here on earth.

Since women have the entire Godhead indwelling in them, along with their immortal male functioning born again spirits joined with Christ, they must have the liberty promised by the Lord (1 Corinthians 3:26; 2 Corinthians 6:16; Ephesians 2:21). "Now the Lord is that Spirit: and where the Spirit of the Lord is, there is liberty" (2 Corinthians 3:17). Kingdom liberty granted to Believers is always balanced with Kingdom responsibility.

Coercive bondage is not part of God's Kingdom. "Thy Kingdom come. Thy will be done on earth as it is in heaven" (Matthew 6:10). If there is no coercive bondage in heaven, then there is not supposed to be involuntary servitude here on earth. On the other hand, the flesh is constantly trying to put Believers in subservient bondage against their consent through habitual sin and addictions. The Lord wants both men and women Believers to willingly and voluntarily submit to the Holy Spirit in service to our Savior and Lord and Believers in His Kingdom.

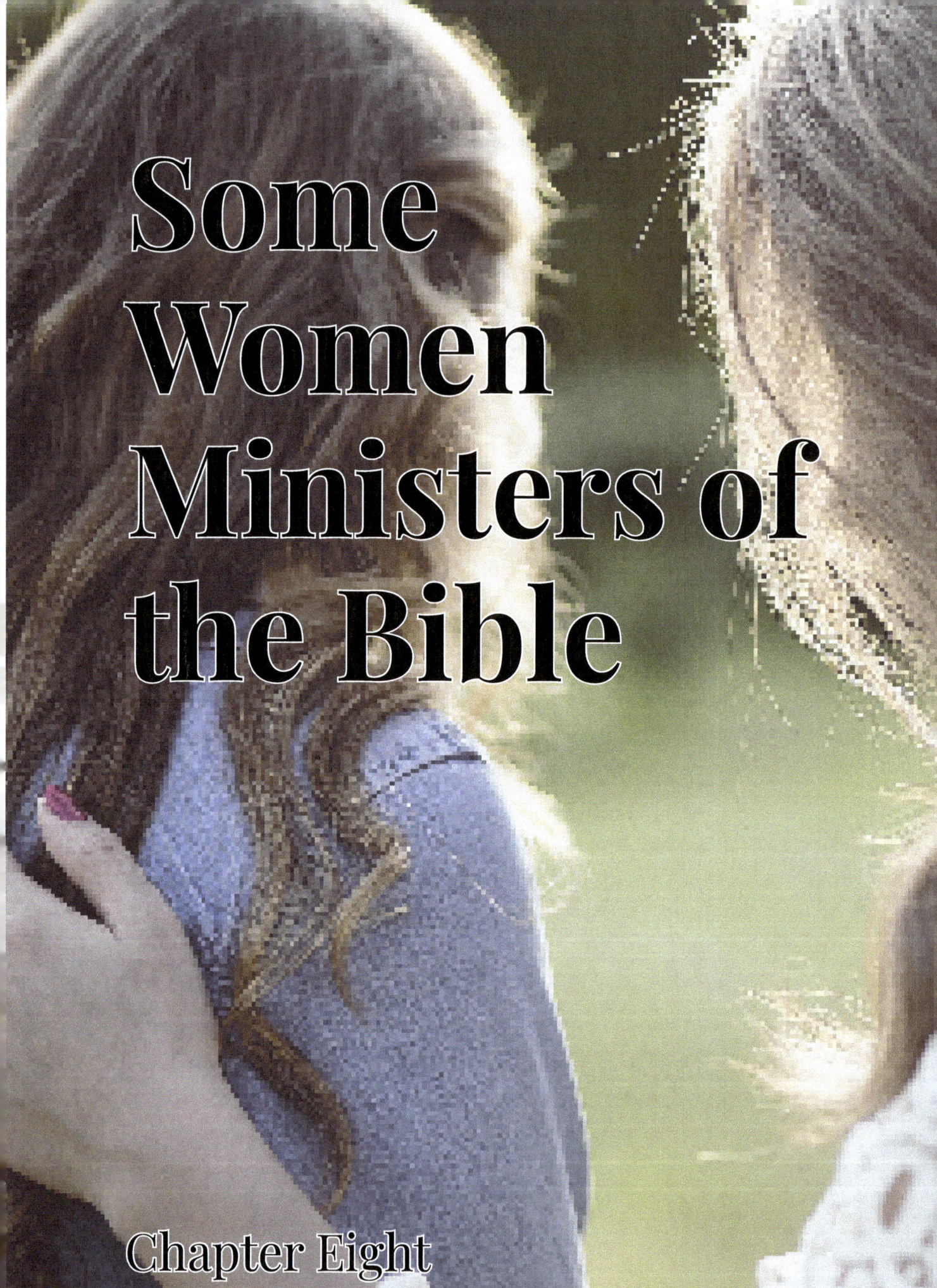

Some Women Ministers of the Bible

Chapter Eight

CHAPTER EIGHT

Some Women Ministers of the Bible

The status in society of the Jewish women has always been above their standing in the Gentile world before Christianity; yet, there was considerably far greater status given to Jewish men as well. Women Believers had a predominantly greater liberty in Christ and in the Kingdom of God.

The Fifth Commandment of the Decalogue commands: "Honor thy father and thy mother: that thy days may be long upon the land which the Lord thy God giveth thee" (Exodus 20:12). This is the first Commandment where the positive results are stated for obeying the commandment, i.e., "that thy days may be long." The word honor means to respect, prize highly, to glorify, and to exalt. Here, God commanded that the father and mother had equal honor, not the father having more honor than the mother.

Colossians 3:20 reiterates the admonition for children to obey. For immature children to learn the ways of the Kingdom, obedience to parents is the key. Obedience is very important to raising godly children. Although the world views obedience as constricting, God says that it is teaching Kingdom principles through discipleship training. Seeking first the Kingdom of God and His righteousness is seeking to be governed by a benevolent and loving King which requires ongoing, daily obedience to the King of kings and His wisdom, knowledge, ways, truth, that brings life. The more you humble yourself and obey, the more authority you are given. It is a Kingdom principle.

When Jesus was coming back to Capernaum, a certain Roman Centurion came to Him, pleading that Jesus heal his servant, who was paralyzed and dreadfully tormented. Matthew 8:7-10, 13, says the principle that obedience relates to faith. "And Jesus saith unto him, 'I will come and heal him.' (8) The centurion answered and said, 'Lord, I am not worthy that thou shouldest come under my roof: but speak the word only, and my servant shall be healed. (9) For I am a man under authority, having soldiers under me: and I say to this man, 'Go,' and he goeth; and to another, 'Come,' and he cometh; and to my servant, 'Do this,' and he doeth it. (10) When Jesus heard it, He marveled, and said to them that followed, 'Verily I say unto you, I have not found so great faith, no, not in Israel.'...... (13) And Jesus said to the Centurion, 'Go thy way; and as thou hast believed, so be it unto thee.' And his servant was healed in the selfsame hour,"

The Roman Centurion had great honor and respect towards Jesus, as the Centurion had heard, and perhaps seen, the wonderful healings done by Jesus. Yet, the Centurion knew that good things get done when soldiers honor and respect the ranking officer's authority. Romans knew respect, honor, and authority that made the Roman Empire what it was. Jesus said this is how faith works - through submission to God's authority.

The relevance here is that when fathers and mothers teach children respect and honor, the children learn to respect authority. Respecting authority is a major key to having great faith in God's Kingdom and obtaining success in business or employment and relationships. So, teaching children to respect authority leads them to have faith in the King in the Kingdom of God.

Likewise, King Lemuel (Solomon) gave a great tribute to women because he had great respect for his mother. Solomon declared that his mother was his teacher (Proverb 31:1) and described her as the model for all women. She is now considered to be the Proverb 31 pattern for all Godly women, especially mothers.

Sarah's name means the mother of nations. God honored Sarah with godly wisdom, and God made Abraham to listen to her wisdom. God commanded Abraham to obey his wife in Genesis 21:12: "And God said unto Abraham, 'Let it not be grievous in thy sight because of the lad (Ishmael), and because of thy bondwoman (Hagar); in all that Sarah hath said unto thee, hearken unto her voice; for in Isaac shall thy seed be called" Sarah knew the will of God; so, God told Abraham to listen to Sarah's wisdom. Sarah and Abraham showed that husbands and wives are to have mutual submission, obedience, and respect in exercising their oneness, with the wives to be the perfect complementary counterpart gift from God to fulfill their joint God-ordained purposes in ministry as a couple. God wants everyone to respect the calling and anointing on another Believer's life. 1 Peter 5:5 says, "Yes, all of you (both women and men) be submissive to one another, and be clothed with humility. . .."

Rebekah was led by the Lord in accepting the proposal to be the wife of a man she had never met, who was Isaac, son of Abraham (Genesis 24:57-58). It is noteworthy that Rebekah's mother and brother told Eleazar, Abraham's servant, that it was Rebekah's decision alone whether to go and marry the prince (Isaac) of a foreign land. Eleazar was a type of the Holy Spirit, who was sent by the father, Abraham, to find a Bride for his son, Isaac. Rebekah exemplified the Ekklesia, today, who must yield to the Holy Spirit to become the Bride of God's only begotten Son.

Rachel and Leah were wives of Jacob, and they were consulted by Jacob for wisdom when he was called by God to return to the land of his fathers to face Essau, whom he had chiseled out of his spiritual inheritance or birthright in exchange for some lentil stew (Genesis 25:29-34) The women advised Jacob to do whatever God commanded him to do (Genesis 31:3-4, 14-16).

Miriam was an older sister of Moses and Aaron and was the sister who watched over the basket of bulrushes in which the baby Moses was laid. In Micah 6:4 God reminds His people: "For I brought you up from the land of Egypt, I redeemed you from the house of bondage; and I sent before you Moses, Aaron and Miriam." Thus, Miriam was declared to be called of God, along with her brothers to deliver His people out of Egypt. Miriam was declared a prophetess of God, "Then Miriam the prophetess, the sister of Aaron, took the timbrel in her hand; and all the women went out after her with timbrels and with dances" (Genesis 15:20).

Deborah was one of the wisest Believers of the Old Testament, chosen by God to be a judge and liberator of God's distressed and defeated people. Deborah was married, the wife of Lapidoth (Judges 4:4), a mother in Israel (Judges 5:7), a Prophetess of Israel. Judges 4:4 says, "Now Deborah, a prophetess, the wife of Lapidoth, was judging Israel at that time." Deborah also was a warrior-leader and judge (Judges 4:6-7, 15-21).

Hannah was the mother of the Prophet, Samuel, whose prayer for a son was granted by God in a mighty way. After her son, Samuel, was weaned, she "lent him to the Lord" (1 Samuel 1:26-28). Then in 1 Samuel 2:1-10, Hannah burst forth in great praise of thanksgiving, and her song became the basis of the Magnificat sung by the Virgin Mary, mother of the Messiah eleven centuries later (Luke 1:46-55).

Abigail recognized that her husband had trespassed God's anointed servant, David. Against her husband's will in favor of the will of God, she sent a large peace offering to appease the anger of David and his men (1 Samuel 25:1-35). David was so impressed with Abigail's wisdom and virtuous nature before the Lord that he made her his wife after her husband's death.

Huldah was a Prophetess for the Kingdom of Judah in a day when most everyone had departed from the Lord. She was led by the Holy Spirit and was known to have given wisdom to rightly discern the things of God. She spoke a prophetic word to a young righteous king, who was King Josiah, who began to do "that which was right before the Lord" (2 Kings 22:2). King Josiah purged Judah and Jerusalem of their pagan idols and burned the bones of the dead pagan priests on the altar. King Josiah discovered the Book of the Law, where he read his name written centuries before, and was motivated to restore the Promise Land and its people to lift up in worship the true God and His righteousness. The high Priest, Hilkiah, did not consult with the prophets Jeremiah, Zephaniah, Nahum, or Habakkuk, who were ministering around Jerusalem at the time. Hilkiah, with four other men, consulted with Huldah, a woman and Prophetess, with whom they had great confidence for her wisdom and the word of the Lord for the nation (2 King 22:14-19).

Queen Esther risked her own life in the office of an Old Testament apostle to deliver her people from certain disaster. "How can I endure to see the evil that shall come unto my people? Or how can I endure to see the destruction of my kindred?" (Esther 8:6). In the heroine's greatest hour, she risked her life to appear before her husband, the Persian king with the decision, "If I perish, I perish" (Esther 4:16). As a result of her and her uncles' faithfulness, Queen Esther and Mordecai were given oversight authority over 127 Persian provinces (Esther 9:29-30).

Many other Great Women were leading Ministers in the Old Testament. Psalm 68:11 reveals the ministry of women who proclaimed the good news: "The Lord gives the command; the women who proclaim the good tidings are a great host." The New King James reveals the feminine gender when it says, "The Lord gave the word: great was the company (Hebrew-tsebaah which is a feminine noun that means "specifically the female mass of people that speak or preach") of those who proclaimed it." The local prejudice of the translators of the King James made them intentionally to disguise that the Scripture says that many women were the proclaimers of the good tidings. In the way it was translated, the word "company" could refer to men. Since the topic in the Psalm pertained to war, then one would understand this reference normally would be to men. To avoid the significance of women in the Old Testament, the translation of this Scripture in several Bible versions fails to mention the feminine gender of the Hebrew noun used.

Mary, Mother of Jesus, was the first of many women, but has the highest stature and prominence among women in the Bible because she was the mother of the King and Savior of the World. As the mother of the Messiah, she participated in the fulfillment of a Godly hope of all virtuous Jewish women. Without question, the greatest honor and favor bestowed upon a fallen human being was given to Mary, a simple, virtuous woman. Mary stood in the office of a Prophetess as she proclaimed in the Magnificat salutation how prophecy of Scripture was being fulfilled with the birth of her Son, the Messiah (Luke 1:46-55). Mary made the announcement of the Great Incarnation. Her song has influenced the women of nations and all of mankind forever. Luke 1:41 says, "And it came to pass, that when Elisabeth heard the salutation of Mary, the babe (John) leaped in her womb; and was filled with the Holy Spirit."

Anna was a Prophetess who prophesied and gave thanks for the coming of baby Jesus as the Lord and spoke of Him. Luke 2:36-38 recognizes Anna the prophetess: "Now there was one, Anna, a prophetess, . . . and this woman was a widow of about eighty-four years, who did not depart from the temple, but served God with fastings and prayers night and day. And coming in that instant she gave thanks to the Lord and spoke of Him to all those who looked for redemption in Jerusalem." Anna did not just minister at the women's meetings but lived and had a public full-time ministry at the temple as a Prophetess and fasted and prayed night and day. Although Anna would not have spoken at the synagogue, where the Jews forbade women speaking, she could have spoken at the Temple, a kind of public auditorium in the theocracy, wherein greater speaking liberty was allowed for women and strangers.

The Samaritan Woman at the Well had the honor of being the first-person Jesus revealed that He was the Messiah, and she became one of the New Testament's first Evangelists through whom a whole city was saved by Christ Jesus (John 4:28-42).

Mary of Bethany was the first to grasp the awesome significance of Jesus'impending death for all mankind; and to this end, she lavishly poured out the precious ointment from her alabaster box on the head, feet, and body of the Savior, which fragrance He would continue to smell in the days ahead when He was left alone, beaten, and crucified (Matthew 26:6-7; 12:1-3). For this act of love and devotion, the Lord said that her sacrifice would be recorded and remembered for all eternity (Matthew 26:12-13).

Many caring Women followed the Lord in his ministry against the public scorn toward women following men with whom they were not married. Luke 8:2-3 gives the following historical account: "And certain women who had been healed of evil spirits and infirmities--Mary called Magdalene, out of whom had come seven demons, and Joanna the wife of Chuza, Herod's steward, and Susanna, and many others who provided for Him from their substance." This was a recorded statement that the women were the ones who provided financial support for the Savior's ministry here on earth.

Daughters of Jerusalem were a reference to the ones who stayed with the Lord during His suffering and crucifixion. Luke 23:27-28 says, "And a great multitude of the people followed Him, and women who also mourned and lamented Him. But Jesus, turning to them, said, 'Daughters of Jerusalem, do not weep for me, but weep for yourselves and for your children.'" There was a Jewish law forbidding the showing of any sympathy to a condemned man. Fearless, these daughters of Jerusalem lamented for their suffering and dying Savior, even at the peril of being arrested and punished for their show of sympathy. To these women, Jesus was not only their Savior and Lord, but also the Great Emancipator of womanhood from the prejudice and bondage of the Eastern and Mid-Eastern cultures.

The Women at the Cross. Most all the men disciples, saved John, fled out of fear of persecution; but the women followers of Jesus did not flee, but stood at the foot of the Cross in front of the Savior; so, He could see them during His suffering and death caused by the Roman crucifixion. Of the men disciples, in Mark 14:50 it is said, "Then they all forsook Him and fled." When the hounds of hell were closing in on the Lamb of God on the Cross, none of the men, save John, stood with Him. However, the women stayed with the Lord until the end of His life here on earth. John 19:25 reveals: "Now there stood by the Cross of Jesus His mother, and his mother's sister, Mary, the wife of Clopas, and Mary Magdalene." Mark 15:40-41 declares, "There were also women looking on from afar, among whom were Mary Magdalene, Mary the mother of James the Less and of Joses, and Salome, who also followed Him and ministered to Him when He was in Galilee, and many other women who came up with Him to Jerusalem." Some of the women watched Jesus' burial (Mark 15:47).

A Woman was chosen to be the first witness of Jesus' resurrection and first witness of Jesus' new creation body. Mary Magdalene was the first to see Jesus in His resurrected newly created body, and she was the first witness to be sent by the Lord to declare His resurrection to the men apostles. John 20:17 reveals, "Jesus said to her, '...Go to My brethren and say to them, 'I am ascending to My Father and your Father, and to My God and your God.'" Mark 16:11 describes the unbelief of the men, "And when they heard that He was alive and had been seen by her, they did not believe." Consequently, it was a woman who was the first Apostle post-resurrection of Jesus Christ.

Jesus called Men and Women to be His Ministers in the Great Commission. Jesus said in Acts 1:8 to both men and women who were there on the mountain witnessing His ascension to heaven, "But ye (both men and women) shall receive power, after that the Holy Ghost is come upon you: and ye (both men and women) shall be witnesses unto Me both in Jerusalem, and in all Judaea, and in Samaria, and unto the uttermost part of the earth." Women Ministers also are called to be Missionaries ministering the gospel of the Kingdom and the message of repentance and remission of sins in other countries.

Women in the Upper Room. Both men and women Believers, including Jesus' Mother and His brothers, were in prayer on the day of Pentecost in the upper room to receive the promised gift of power of the Holy Spirit to enable them to be the Lord's witnesses throughout the world. Acts 1:13-14 gives the following account of the beginning of the Ekklesia: "And when they were come in, they went up into an upper room, where abode both Peter, and James, and John, and Andrew, Philip, and Thomas, Bartholomew, and Matthew, James the son of Alphaeus, and Simon Zelotes, and Judas the brother of James. (14) These all continued with one accord in prayer and supplication, with the women, and Mary the mother of Jesus, and with his brethren." Acts 2:4 says, "And they were all (both men and women) filled with the Holy Spirit and began to speak with other tongues, as the Spirit gave them utterance." The outpouring of the Holy Spirit was upon both men and women. Then Peter stood up and explained to those watching and listening of this great visit by the Holy Spirit, saying in Acts 2:17-18, "And it shall come to pass in the last days, saith God, I will pour out of my Spirit upon all flesh: and your sons and your daughters shall prophesy, and your young men shall see visions, and your old men shall dream dreams: (18)And on my servants and on my handmaidens I will pour out in those days of my Spirit; and they shall prophesy'" Both young men and women are chosen by the Holy Spirit to prophesy in the endtime Joel 2 revival. Why do some religious leaders forbid women to prophesy now, and some don't accept prophecy as a gift in the Ekklesia at this time?

In the First Century Ekklesia, Women Believers were allowed to pray, prophesy, preach, teach, and witness.

There was and is no distinction between men and women regarding salvation, the graces, and spiritual gifts of the Father, Word/Son, and Holy Spirit (Galatians 3:28; Romans 12; 1 Corinthians 12; Ephesians 4).

Both Men and Women labored with Paul. Paul in Romans 16:1-15 lists both men and women working together preaching the gospel: Phoebe, a businesswoman, Priscilla, a fellow worker of Paul, Mary, "who labored much for us," "Philologus and Julia, Nereus and his sister."

Philip had four daughters who were Prophets. Acts 21:8-9 says "And the next day we that were of Paul's company departed and came unto Caesarea: and we entered the house of Philip the evangelist, which was one of the seven; and abode with him. (9) And the same man had four daughters, virgins, which did prophesy."

Those Women Ministers who labored with Paul. Likewise, Paul in Philippians 4:3 urges: "And I urge you also true companion, help these women who labored with me in the gospel."

In the Book of Acts, 33 women Believers are mentioned who suffered persecution the same as men Believers. Saul, before his conversion, persecuted women as well as men for preaching the gospel of the Kingdom and repentance and remission of sin. Acts 8:3 reveals the actions of Saul: "As for Saul, he made havoc of the church, entering every house, and dragging off men and women, committing them to prison." Acts 9:1-2 continues Saul's actions: "And Saul yet breathing out threatenings and slaughter against the disciples of the Lord, went unto the High Priest, (2) And desired of him letters to Damascus to the synagogues, that if he found any of this Way, whether they were men or women, he might bring them bound unto Jerusalem." Later, Saul was named Paul, and he testified of his conversion in Acts 22:4, "And I persecuted this Way unto the death, binding and delivering into prisons both men and women." Women and men together suffered for their faith, including imprisonment and death, so the first century men and women were persecuted severely for preaching the gospel of the Kingdom and repentance and remission of sin.

Acts 9:4-5 speaks of when Paul was on the road to Damascus when the Lord interrupted Saul's journey, "And he (Saul) fell to the earth, and heard a voice saying unto him, 'Saul, Saul, why persecutest thou me?' (5) And he (Saul) said, 'Who art thou, Lord?' And the Lord said, 'I am Jesus whom thou persecutest: it is hard for thee to kick against the pricks.'"

When Jesus asked why Saul was persecuting Him, Jesus was referring to persecution of His body, consisting of both men and women, not just the men alone. Women's spiritual liberation in the Kingdom of God is manifested based on the lives of the women martyrs, just like the men. Therefore, the blood of both the women and the men martyrs have been spilt for preaching the gospel of the Kingdom and repentance and remission of sins. If the women are equal in suffering, they are equal in Ministry calling and honor.

Dorcas was a devout woman who was "full of good works and charitable deeds which she did" and was well known for her ministry to the poor and needy, a sortof "Mother Theresa" of her time. The Holy Spirit through Peter raised her from the dead which caused many people to believe in the Lord (Acts 9:36-42).

Lydia is credited as being the first convert in Europe. She was a businesswoman who made and sold purple fabric, and she received the Gospel from Paul in Philippi (Acts 16:13-15). Under Jewish law, a synagogue had to be established when there was a population of at least ten men in a community. Since there was an absence of a synagogue, this small group of women prayer warriors were given the task of praying in the first Christian Ekklesia for the whole western world.

Euodia and Syntyche were also women in the Philippian Ekklesia who helped Paul in spreading the gospel (Philippians 4:2-3).

There were many other women Minsters. These Godly women in the New Testament included Tryphena and Tryphosa who labored with Paul (Romans 16:12); the mother of Rufus, whom Paul claim to be like a mother to him (Romans 16:13); Apphia (Philemon 2); Claudia (2 Timothy 4:21); "of the chief women not a few," and "honorable women which were Greeks" (Acts 17:4,12); Lois and Eunice, grandmother and mother of Timothy, whose continuous teaching of the Holy Scriptures gave him a solid foundation for ministry (2 Timothy 1:5; 3:15).

Finally, Paul salutes Junia who was of "note among the apostles" (Romans 16:7). The Greek for note is episemos, which means "highly regarded, remarkable, eminent, and notable." Thus, Junia was a highly anointed and gifted woman of God who was ordained and functioned in the office of an Apostle. Thus, it was not only men that functioned as Apostles.

Cultural prejudices against Women

Chapter Nine

CHAPTER NINE

Cultural Prejudices Against Women

The religious cultures in the United States, Great Britain, Canada, Central and South America, and Europe historically have demeaned Christian women. Likewise, the men in the Asian cultures historically have degraded Asian women. Certain non-Christian religious groups, such as some Islamic fundamentalist cultures, historically have treated women as subservient to men. To be thorough, these Islamic fundamentalist cultures have been very restrictive to the men as well in the practice of their religion.

Consequently, the statements made in this book are directed to all the male dominated societies and religions, but particularly to the male-dominated Christian cultures in the Western world, which need to re-examine their prejudices and motives concerning the biblical status of women as qualified and legitimate Ministers the same as men. Gender was never, and is not now, not a barrier toward being a Minister. Qualifying or disqualifying a man or woman based upon the wrong gender is unbiblical and at worse, it is helping the devil by disqualifying women as Kingdom Ambassadors of Christ, Kingdom Soldiers, kings, lords, and priests. Disqualifying women as Ministers are decisions based purely upon the flesh, as this book postulates and establishes by the authority of scripture.

The point made is the subjugation of women has been in every society and culture, and it still is a problem in some cultures more than others in the world. This prejudice against women has come into the Ekklesia that attacks the liberties and freedoms afforded all Believers, regardless of race, culture, age, or gender. No Ekklesia culture is exempt, and none can say they historically have not relegated women to some degree as an inferior position, such as teaching only children or other women, and cooking for, fellowship gatherings.

In the United States, we have seen the women lash out in the natural with the Women's Liberation Movement since the 1960's, but the problem is more spiritual than natural; and there are greater issues other than equal pay, equal promotion, or women keeping their maiden name after marriage.

In some areas of conflict between men and women Believers, the problem is also demonic, but the factors involved is complicated. It takes much spiritual insight to see clearly through the murky waters of Ekklesia structure and religious tradition. The Ekklesia leaders have been lagging, and the other problem is that many women in the various religious denominations still support the man-centered idea that somehow men are superior to women in spiritual calling and anointing to be an Ephesians 4:11 minister, which has little or no biblical support.

When I came back to the Lord, I suspected but did not know the problem of discrimination against women as Ephesians 4:11 Ministers was so rampant, as I thought everyone in the current Ekklesia culture believed that women were equally accepted as Ministers the same as men in ministry. I discovered this anti-women prejudice in public ministry is still a problem in the many denominations today. My research brought me great surprise since I thought everyone honored the anointing of the Holy Spirit regardless of the person ministering, whether a man or a woman.

Men and women alike in the old religious order still tell me that they do not believe that a woman could be a pastor over a man because of the potential problem with improper intimacy during counseling. I asked them, "Then how can a man be a Pastor who counsels women alone in his office if the purpose of ruling out women as Pastor is to avoid the improper intimacy of men with women?"

Is not Christ Jesus, and God in His triune nature, primarily male in nature? Are we Believers, both man and woman, Christ's bride? They would respond, "Well, I believe it is okay for a man to be a Pastor of a woman, but not a woman to be a Pastor of a man." They really had no concrete reasoning, but just had the tradition of their religious denomination they were espousing, which seems to have made void the commandments of God in their lives concerning the activation of women as Ephesians 4:11 Ministers.

I showed them in Scripture where the immortal female functioning soul in every person, in the spiritual realm, is female in function, the new, immortal male functioning born again spirit is male in function, and the mortal male functioning body is male in function. I told them that even under their religious doctrine that a woman could pastor a man because anyone under the anointing is expressing the immortal male functioning born again spirit and the male functioning of the Holy Spirit, as there are proper ways to avoid any impropriety, such as having another pastor or the Pastor's spouse present when counseling the opposite gender. Hence, it should not make a difference whether a person is a woman or man who is ministering since under the anointing of the Holy Spirit, and as we have seen in Scripture, there is no distinction between a man and a woman in the spiritual realm regarding ministry (Galatians 3:28).

Sinful intimacy between men and women in Ekklesia is an unfortunate fact, but some have used the possibility of displaced affections to exclude women from the counseling ministry. I do recognize that some male Ministers have fallen from grace in history because of counseling women alone. To avoid wrongful intimacy is a good reason why women should also be pastors or other Ministers instead of using the reason to exclude women from ministry. Husbands and wives should stay under the authoritative covering of their marriage by the couple ministering together when the Believer who requests ministry counseling is of the opposite gender. Women Pastors can minister to men, and men Pastors can minister to women; but both should do it with proper authoritative covering to avoid impropriety or the appearance thereof.

Men and women Pastors should use his or her spouse in the event he or she has the practice of laying hands on the opposite gender in the intimate areas of the person's body requesting healing, as when women and men are being prayed for healing of reproductive problems. If a male or female minister is not married, then another husband or wife who are co-Ministers should be present to help minister to avoid the appearance of any impropriety. Everything should be done decently and in order as to not violate the social customs of the culture or general standards of gentility or at least attempt to convey or maintain the appearance of refinement and proper protocol.

Yet, to say that men cannot minister to women, or vice versa, would exclude Jesus from ministering to the Samaritan woman at the well who was chosen as the first person He revealed Himself as the Messiah, or forgiving the woman caught in adultery, the casting out demons in Mary Magdalene, or healing the woman with an issue of blood.

To correct the practices that exclude women from ministry is the job of those Ministers who function primarily in the apostolic and prophetic foundational ministry engiftments as this is a foundational error in the Ekklesia.

There are scriptures that were and still are misused by historical religious leaders in both the Catholic and Protestant movements. I have done a thorough study, looking up the Greek where English was translated, and it shows the falsity of relegating women to disqualification from leadership ministry just because of their gender.

Why can't there be a female Pope? Why do many of the nation's largest denominations do not ordain women or allow them to lead congregations. Where is the scripture that says women are disqualified from leadership due to their gender? That was not God's punishment that God declared to Eve after she ate the forbidden fruit in the Garden in Genesis 3:16. Instead, Eve was given the honor of having one of her posterities, which was the Virgin Mary that out of her womb came the Savior of the world. Adam honored his wife by naming her "Eve," which means the mother of the living, not the mother of the dying. Who can deny the sacrificial work of the ministry of Mother Teresa for example?

Many religious denomination doctrines do not recognize women as Pastors or Elders or leaders. Yet, some religious denomination doctrines allow senior women to oversee the women's department, which is an auxiliary ministry of the religious denomination. Some religious denominations were founded by women, but later the leadership became predominately men Pastors and leaders. What religious tradition or idea neutralized the calling of the woman founder of these denominations?

Other religious denominations believe in the spiritual gifting of all Believers, but the denomination teaches that women are not to take positions of pastoral or elder leadership within their old religious order. Rather, they allow women to teach other women, show hospitality, evangelize, and serve in other aspects of ministry, but not as the Pastor or Elder.

Ministers who have the apostolic and prophetic functions are called to put foundational beliefs in order in the body of Christ (Ephesians 2:20). God wants to deliver a Believer's immortal female functioning soul of generational and cultural evil spirits, lusts of the flesh, lusts of the eyes, pride of life, along with family curses that have been handed down to the third and fourth generations. Believers are directed that while in their prayer closets that they should daily plead the curse removing benefits through the power of the Cross of Calvary in their lives (Galatians 3:13-14).

Why is there subjugation of women in the Ekklesia (kingdom government assembly and military assembly) that stops Believers from entering the Kingdom of God where subjugation of women is forbidden by God? The problem is that people sometimes victimize others the same way they were victimized. The resultant trauma becomes a doorway for fleshly and demonic activity. Galatians 5:13 says, "For, brethren, ye have been called unto liberty; only use not liberty for an occasion to the flesh, but by love serve one another."

Galatians 5:16-21 says, "This I say then, 'Walk in the spirit (born again spirit under the authority of the Holy Spirit), and ye shall not fulfill the lust of the flesh. (17) For the flesh lusteth against the spirit (born again spirit), and the spirit against the flesh: and these are contrary the one to the other: so that ye (exercising your will in your soul) cannot do the things that ye would. (18) But if ye (your soul) be led of the spirit, ye are not under the law. (19) Now the works of the flesh are manifest, which are these; Adultery, fornication, uncleanness, lasciviousness, (20) idolatry, witchcraft, hatred, variance, emulations, wrath, strife, seditions, heresies, (21 envyings, murders, drunkenness, reveling, and such like: of the which I tell you before, as I have also told you in time past, that they which do such things shall not inherit the kingdom of God."

Any injustice done to a person often becomes the excuse to do injustice to others. Yet, this iniquity that becomes the curse of the law can be stopped from passing to the next generations of the Believer's posterity by pleading the benefits of Jesus being crucified and dying on the Roman Cross. The Believer must enter in the crucifixion of Christ Jesus to experience the liberation of the resurrection life of Christ (Galatians 3:13;

Romans 6:6; Galatians 2:20). These generational iniquities (habits of sinning) become cultural iniquities allowing the curse of the law to manifest in Believers' lives, which distinguishes one culture and one family from another. Believers must accept the truth that a wrong done is not a justification to do wrong to others.

Thieves usually justify their actions by the fact that they, themselves, have had things stolen from them. Violent men and women usually have been victims of violence. This principle is why Jesus taught that people should not take revenge against another. Jesus taught throughout the Gospels to forgive others even as you have been forgiven; so, that injustice will not come back on you and cause you to be a perpetrator. In fact, Jesus taught in Mark 11:25-26 that faith cannot work if the person has unforgiveness in his or her heart, and without faith it is impossible to please God (Hebrews 11:6).

Christ is the Head of His body, which makes the Head male in nature (Ephesians 1:22-23). On the other hand, the Ekklesia, representing the body of Christ is also the future Bride of Christ. So, the Ekklesia has a female nature as well. Again, it deserves repeating over and over that in the spiritual realm there is no distinction between male and female as far as ministry is concerned, but a oneness of both male and female (Galatians 3:28).

Romans 8:15 clearly declares the absolute liberation of all Believers, not just the men. "For you have not received a spirit of slavery leading to fear again, but you have received a spirit of adoption as sons by which we cry out, 'Abba Father!'" Therefore, slavery is beneath the creative dignity of both men and women. Since the essence of both men and women Believers is the immortal male functioning born again spirit; then when the word of God refers to men and women as sons of God as in Romans 8:15, it is a reference to the immortal male functioning born again spirit. Thus, women Believers should not think that the Bible is only a male gender book.

The problem involved is in the tendency of fallen man, caused by the enslavement of all mankind by Satan, to try to take dominion over God's highest creation, made in the image and likeness of His Son, which creation, man, was made and designed by God only to be a ruler of the creation, not a ruler of other people, and certainly not a slave. In Genesis 1:26, the male man and female man were both made in the image and likeness of God and were mandated jointly the work of taking dominion of all other living creatures, but not other human beings (Genesis 1:27-28). Thus, the enslavement by any human being of another human being is inherently against God's created order.

Unfortunately, people in every culture have not completely escaped from the desire to enslave other human beings or classes of people. As with slavery based on race, treating women as chattel or personal tangible property is also a form of cultural slavery based on gender. Although legislation has been enacted in government and decided in judicial cases concerning job-related gender discrimination and sexual abuse, women in society in many cultures are still perceived as being inherently inferior to men contrary to biblical proscription. Slavery or coercive bondage is against God's principles and mandate for His Kingdom. Spousal abuse is still a very real problem in the United States, and elsewhere in the world. Hitting a wife to force submission is the highest form of dishonor to both the wife and husband. Nothing hinders a husband's prayers more than physically abusing his wife (1 Peter 3:7).

Galatians 5:1 proclaims: "Stand fast therefore in the liberty wherewith Christ hath made us free and be not entangled again with the yoke of bondage." John 8:36 says, "If the Son therefore shall make you free, ye shall be free indeed."

Slavery, bondage, or subjugation of any group of people is wrong in any culture. The Kingdom of God does not sanction slavery, involuntary bondage, or subjugation as a viable biblical principle or lifestyle in the Kingdom of God. Romans 8:2-3 declares: "For the law of the Spirit of life in Christ Jesus hath made me free from the law of sin and death. For what the law could not do, in that it was weak through the flesh, God sending his own Son in the likeness of sinful flesh, and for sin, condemned sin in the flesh."

Believers cannot walk away from the biblical truth just because they have been victimized. Believers can take the ownership and possession of the problem resulting from the trauma of being a victim without taking the guilt of causing the problem. If they do confront their problems then they develop bravery. When I was a child I lived on a farm. My grandfather taught me how to kill snakes, so, I did not fear snakes. John 8: 31-32 declares Jesus' liberating proclamation: "Then said Jesus to those Jews which believed on him, 'If ye continue in my word, then are ye My disciples, indeed; and ye shall know the truth, and the truth shall make you free.'" This was Jesus' promise of liberty from man-made religion. The Bible does not contain the establishment of religion but demands relationship directly with the Savior and the Godhead.

Generally, false religion has motivated more mass killings than any other reasons. Obedience to Jesus' words means you know the Truth, and by knowing the Truth is experiencing the freedom Jesus brought to earth from religious bondage. Those who know how it feels to be victims of bondage should be the forerunners of the proponents of biblical liberation of all people, whether a man or woman.

All too often, the problems in a particular culture are brought into the Ekklesia to solve, but these particular problems are assimilated into the Ekklesia to make the new Believer feel at home with acceptance of his or her cultural traditions. Sometimes, these cultural and generational iniquities are prejudices or weaknesses which demonic spirits use to bring temptation and hold the people in sin to rob them of the liberty for which

Christ suffered and died. Letting go of cultural inequities is part of knowing the biblical truth that leads to liberty. The Kingdom of God has a spiritual culture that trumps all other cultures. The cultural injustices can become religious doctrines of bondage when men and women incorrectly translate, interpret, and apply Scripture to further their cultural prejudices.

To this same end, we must pray against the prejudices in the body of Christ, which have subjugated women. Works of the flesh along with demonic religious spirits have influenced good men to take Scriptural passages out of context to influence the body of Christ in their denominations to further these cultural prejudices against women.

Satan hates women because the first woman became the mother of the Seed Who crushed his headship and destroyed the work Satan wrought in the Garden of Eden in the complete deprivation of mankind for many, many generations, (Genesis 3; 1 John 3:8).

Since the cultural bias against women is readily apparent in all cultures, all cultures around the globe have similar histories, and the prejudices or cultural tendencies to make women an inferior group based on the gender is of the flesh and not the Spirit of God. This gender prejudice and subjugation has come into the old religious order structures that are cemented in their foundational doctrines that need to change. These false religious doctrines are manmade, not ordained of God. These false religious doctrines have stymied the mandated mission of the Ekklesia, (Matthew 28:18-20).

The greatest reason why this scheme by demonic religious spirits, working through the temptations of the flesh, against the women has been so strong in the old religious order structures has been to keep the most important woman, the Betrothed of Christ, from coming forth in her full stature and glory. Religion keeps the Betrothed locked up in a Tower built by cultural anti-women prejudices.

Consequently, one can easily see how and why Scripture has been misinterpreted, mistranslated, and mis-applied through the influence of demonic religious spirits who have found agreement with cultural demons and macho works of the flesh to keep women out of ministry.

Women could be the best teachers of the men as to how to be more like the Betrothed of Christ. When the men finally accept their female function ultimately as Christ's Bride to be, then the Betrothed of Christ will be loosed in all her glory! The biblical liberation of women in the body of Christ to be Ministers will be one of the first steps in God's great end-time revival.

It was not a woman who sold Jesus for thirty pieces of silver. The women disciples did not flee in the garden of Gethsemane when Jesus was arrested. Although Peter denied Jesus three times after Jesus' arrest, not one of the women disciples denied Him. When all the men, save John, abandoned Jesus Who was whipped and crucified, the women stayed with Jesus while He was dying on the Roman Cross.

The women followed Jesus' body when it was taken to the tomb. Similarly, a woman (Mary Magdalene) was the first person to witness the Resurrected Lord in His new creation body and the first to witness Jesus had risen from the dead. Mary Magdalene gave the first message after the Lord was resurrected when Jesus sent her to the men Apostles where to meet Him. To the credit of women, none of the women deserted, betrayed, or denied the Lord. Women were the ones who ministered to the Lord and supported Him from their substance. It was a woman who washed the Lord's feet with her tears, while another spent all she had for a fragrant ointment to anoint Jesus' head and body for His burial. While most all the men were fleeing in fear of their lives, the women stayed weeping, wailing, and lamenting for the Lamb of God while He was being slain.

Wherever the Gospel has spread since Jesus' crucifixion, it has been the message of not only the emancipation of women but also the liberty for all mankind who accept Jesus as Lord and Savior. All Believers, both men women, equally are delivered from the bondage of infernal death and the bondage of sin unto eternal life. God the Word, Jesus' divine nature's presence evokes all the latent and tender mercies for all mankind that women were born with greater sensitive natures.

Jesus' purpose for coming to earth was manifold but included seeking a multi-Believers Betrothed and later multi-Believers' Bride. Jesus' beginning started here on earth with a woman and mother from whom the Messiah and Savior of the world was born. Jesus died on a Roman Cross for the love of His Betrothed and future Bride. It will be a woman and Bride for whom the Lord is returning to reign with Him as His Ekklesia and Queen throughout eternity (Revelation 5:10; Revelation chapters 21&22).

We men can learn a lot from Ephesians 4:11 women Ministers and our wives and other women servants in the Ekklesia. We Believer men can receive an impartation from Believer women how to express love, emotion, sensitivity, servanthood to others, patience, caring, comfort, and above all else, how to have submission to Christ Jesus as His Betrothed and future Bride in God's redemptive Kingdom order and plan. Jesus is coming back soon for His Betrothed; so, we Believer men better learn from the Believer women how to be the Betrothed of Christ.

Romans 13:11 warns: "And do this, knowing the time, that now it is high time to awake out of sleep; for now, our salvation is nearer than when we first believed."
First the natural, then the spiritual! We have seen the Communist Iron Curtain come down in 1990. This was a

major spiritual wall which allowed the truth of the Gospel to come into many atheistic countries heretofore unreachable by mainstream Christianity. In the same manner, we need to bring down the walls of spiritual subjugation of women in the true Ekklesia when it comes to ministry; so, the Holy Spirit can bring revival or awakening without restriction.

Satan! Your evil plot is being exposed! The Lord rebukes you Satan! We, as Christ's multi-Believers Betrothed, oppose you in the name of Jesus! As Christ's Betrothed and spiritual Army in God's Kingdom, we put on our combat boots, take up our spiritual weapons and armor (2 Corinthians 10:4-5; Ephesians 6:10-18), and now we Believers, both men and women, use God's rhema word as the Sword of the Spirit to cut the roots of the tree of the knowledge of good and evil that has culturally kept the Betrothed of Christ in bondage.

To the glory of Christ and His Body, we join the Captain of the Host to tear down the walls of prejudice and discrimination that have divided the Lord's Ekklesia. Through the power of the Holy Spirit, we finish the eradication of the false class system ignorantly established by men Ministers against women being Ministers for the last 1800 years or so. With the authority given to the Lord by our heavenly Father, and the authority of Jesus Christ has given to His disciples as Ambassadors and Soldiers of the Kingdom of God (Matthew 28:18; 2 Corinthians 5:20; 2 Timothy 2:3-4), we join Christ in rebuking the kingdom of darkness that is resisting the Betrothed of Christ from coming forth in all of her radiant glory as the Bride of Christ to shine forth with wisdom, knowledge, understanding, spiritual kingdom authority, and beauty to proclaim the gospel of the Kingdom of God, the message of repentance and remission of sins, that bring people exiled in the world into God's temple and Kingdom with righteousness, peace, and joy in the Holy Spirit.

When Christ's Betrothed is freed from bondage, she will become Christ's Bride, and fulfill the bridal paradigm to join the Holy Spirit and proclaim, "And the Spirit and the Bride say, 'Come'" (Revelation 22:17).

Conclusion and Exhortation

CONCLUSION AND EXHORTATION

I commend all the women Ministers who have been fighting the battle for recognition in the true Ekklesia as chosen and anointed Ephesians 4:11 Ministers. However, these women leaders cannot do it all, and they need all the truth-seeking support of women and men of God in this next great awakening of the Spirit of God.

It is time that the women, especially in America, change their focus from just seeking equality in the job market for equal pay just to exist in their time here on earth with greater ease. Like men, women need to take their focus off money and self-esteem and focus on submitting to the will of the Holy Spirit and seek first the Kingdom of God and His righteousness (Matthew 6:33).

Women Believers need to come out of their spiritual slumber, complacency, and apathy and stand up and rally behind the women and men Believer leaders in the true Ekklesia through whom God is revealing women's true stature in the word of God as kings, lords, priests, ambassadors, and soldiers in the kingdom of God.

The Holy Spirit is calling forth the women Believers en mass to reveal the true loving, caring, comforting, servanthood of the Betrothed, as being both men and women Believers. Women Believers who learn how to make herself ready before going into the world need to spiritually teach the spiritual beautification of holiness to men Believers going into the world. Mature spiritual women of God need to teach men how to make ready for the Bridegroom Who is returning back to earth to rule and reign with Believers throughout eternity (Daniel 7:14, 22, 27). Women Believers know more about how to take care of the problems of spots and wrinkles than the men Believers. Women Believers have learned how to make the Betrothed spiritually beautiful through worship of God and intercessory prayer.

Women Believers are often quicker to submit to the Lord than the men Believers. There are more women Believes that are in the Kingdom of God or Ekklesia than men Believers. If the devil succeeds in disqualifying women Believers from being Ephesians 4:11 Ministers, then without a battle, he has removed 55% of the Kingdom Ambassadors and Kingdom Soldiers that would come up against his kingdom of darkness and interfere with his rule of the world system. When the devil convinced women Believers to worship self as an idol instead of God, then, again, he succeeded to rid the Kingdom of God of more warriors that would come up against his kingdom. When the devil convinced women that they own their own bodies, instead God owning their bodies; then, the devil convinced women that killing a fetus growing in the women's womb was not human being and therefore not murder if killed. Abortion wiped out more humans in the name of freedom and responsibility.

I challenge women Believers to listen especially to the mature women leaders in the Ekklesia who have been laying down their lives as forerunners before the Spirit's outpouring of His purpose, power, and love in revival and awakening to abolish the slothfulness of the body of Christ in the Ekklesia.

God is pouring out His Spirit on all flesh, "... and your sons and your daughters shall prophesy ... and also upon the (male) servants and upon the handmaids in those days I will pour out My Spirit" (Joel 2:28-29). The Holy Spirit is being poured out on both the sons and daughters, not just the sons, and pouring out His Spirit on the male servants and the handmaids, not just the male servants. Since this is a prophetic word about the future revival, then it would behoove the male and female leaders in the traditional religious orders to get their traditions and doctrines in line with the word of God and not the religious traditions that make void the commandments of God. Since God chose women to be joint Ministers with men from the time of creation of mankind, then why have leaders of old religious orders decided to change God's original creation mandate for women Believers whose sins are forgiven and are no longer in a fallen state?

Women Believers, the word of God challenges you to follow the footsteps of the brave and bold women Ministers who have been led by the Holy Spirit to blazon the trail through the wilderness temptations of the devil and the religious strongholds that exist in some old religious order structures that want to hold on to their religious traditions. Following the examples of these truth-seeking women leaders of God, do not listen to the voice of the devil, the voices of this fallen world, or the voices of religious tradition. Do not put yourself in marital, economic, or social bondage. On the other hand, do not follow the anti-man ideas of the rebellious humanistic and secular Women's Liberation Movement that has sown a mixed seed. Following the lead of these Godly women Ministers, be led by the Spirit of the Lord; for "... where the Spirit of the Lord is there is liberty" (2 Corinthians 3:17).

In conclusion, let's look at a very motivating scripture passages. Isaiah 32: 9-10,15-18 motivates, "Rise up, ye women that are at ease; hear My voice, ye careless daughters; give ear unto My speech. Many days and years shall ye be troubled, ye careless women: for the vintage shall fail, the gathering shall not come. . . Until the Spirit be poured upon us from on high, and the wilderness be a fruitful field, and the fruitful field be counted for a forest. Then judgment shall dwell in the wilderness, and righteousness remain in the fruitful field. And the work of righteousness shall be peace, and the effect of righteousness quietness and assurance forever. And My people shall dwell in a peaceable habitation, and in sure dwellings, and in quiet resting places."

Thanks for the great women of God who are bold enough to reject religion in favor of intimate relationship as the Betroth of the Lord. They are like the five wise virgins who keep their lamps full of the anointing oil that illuminates the light to see the Bridegroom coming. These women are not intimidated in going into the marketplace as professionals and businesswomen to maintain their lamps full of oil. These great women of God have an honorable place in the Kingdom of God, even though some of the traditional religious order leaders yet do not see them as Kingdom Ministers or they relegate them to a confined ministry instead of the freedom of being led by the Holy Spirit.

Women Believers, you are called of God to be Ministers, so it is time for Women Ministers Awaken!

BIO
Dr. Nova Dean Pack

Dr. Nova Dean Pack's father left the family when he was 3 years old, and at age 10 his mother died at age 32, leaving six children behind. Dr. Pack and his brothers and sisters were raised on his grandparents' farm where there was continuous hard work as chores - taking care of 120 acres, along with feeding many cows, pigs, chickens, ducks, geese, and other animals and milking two to three cows morning and night, along with yearly soil preparation, seed planting, cultivating, the harvesting of hay and crops. For solace, on the farm, was a beautiful wooded area where Dr. Pack spent many hours alone praying and seeking God and reading his bible. The farm life was very tough, but the work ethic was engrained in Dr. Pack's foundation of beliefs. Southern Illinois was part of the Bible Belt; so, most everyone went to an old religious order as a lifestyle, although it was mostly a religious experience.

After his mother died, Dr. Pack, at age 11 was born again and had a very intimate relationship with Jesus and the Holy Spirit. He taught Sunday School from the Bible to other students near his age and baptized several people his age and younger in the creeks of Illinois at age 13 and onward.

Dr. Pack moved to California at age 15. He worked his way through college and graduated from Cal State University Long Beach in 1971. He graduated from Pepperdine University School of Law, a fundamental Christian based top rated law school, in 1974. He passed the State Bar exam on the first sitting also in 1974. He immediately started practicing law with other partners, but he left the partnership and started his sole practice of law in 1981.

Dr. Pack personally was ordained by two known prophets in California in 1992; namely Dr. Chuck Flynn and Dr. Richard Maiden. Dr. Pack received ordination papers with the Independent Assemblies of God International (IAOGI), Santa Ana, CA in 1993 and has been the corporate attorney for IAOGI since that year. Dr. Pack was the Senior Pastor of a Church fellowship from 1994 through 1999 in Redlands, CA. Dr. Pack was overseer of two ministries from 1993 through 2020 and ministered monthly at those ministries, along with other *Ekklesia*. In 2004, the Holy Spirit inspired Dr. Pack to use the name "Biblitarian," so Dr. Pack formed the ministry called "Biblitarian Ministries."

Dr. Pack broadcasted a radio talk show entitled "Business in Ministry" in San Bernardino, CA., for two years from 1992 through 1994 where he taught business men and women how to make their businesses a place of ministry. In 1994 through 1996, Dr. Pack taught a daily radio teaching that aired in Riverside and San Bernardino Counties, California, where his ongoing sermons in Church became the subjects of radio broadcasts.

During this period, Dr. Pack conducted monthly teachings for 50 straight weeks at several *Ekklesia*, teaching men and women that their businesses were their venue of ministry. Dr. Pack sees his law practice as a place and opportunity for ministry to those in need, where he witnesses to the unsaved, prays for the sick, takes care of those in need, and educates his clients and employees on the Biblical principles of business and economics and estate planning. Dr. Pack is one of the very few attorneys at law that actually brings the wisdom and principles in the Bible into his law practice for the benefit of his Christian clients and all those seeking his advice.

Dr. Pack is a prolific writer, having written over 30 Christian books on various spiritual topics (most of which have not, as yet, been published), some directly for the Believer in business. Also, he is an accomplished public minister who teaches under a strong anointing. Dr. Pack has learned how to bring the dynamic of intellectual endeavor under the authority and anointing of the Holy Spirit. He has preached and taught more than a thousand messages over the years.

Dr. Pack's ministry focus is preaching the gospel of the Kingdom (Matthew 24:14) and the message of repentance and remission of sins (Luke 24:27), which Jesus commanded to be the dual priority of preaching and teaching. He also is an inciteful teacher in the transformation of the soul and how to bring biblical wisdom, knowledge, and understanding for practical use in daily living.

Dr. Pack sends his regular teachings to Believers in over 65 different countries. Dr. Pack currently broadcasts his podcasts under the name "Biblitarian Ministries" on the priority of seeking first the Kingdom of God and His righteousness, God's grace extended for repentance and remission of sins, and the receiving of benefits of living in the Kingdom of God. Biblitarian Ministries can be viewed on The Marketplace Network, a Christian media network broadcasting on Amazon Fire TV, Facebook, YouTube and Twitter platforms. Dr. Pack may be contacted at ***packnovapack@aol.com.***